All About Sahara Desert: A Kid's Guide to the World's Largest Hot Desert

Educational Books For Kids, Volume 8

Shah Rukh

Published by Shah Rukh, 2024.

While every precaution has been taken in the preparation of this book, the publisher assumes no responsibility for errors or omissions, or for damages resulting from the use of the information contained herein.

ALL ABOUT SAHARA DESERT: A KID'S GUIDE TO THE WORLD'S LARGEST HOT DESERT

First edition. September 18, 2024.

Copyright © 2024 Shah Rukh.

ISBN: 979-8224010974

Written by Shah Rukh.

Table of Contents

Prologue...1

Chapter 1: The Origins of the Sahara Desert 2

Chapter 2: Wildlife in the Sahara's Sands 6

Chapter 3: The Sahara's Famous Sand Dunes....................11

Chapter 4: Ancient Civilizations of the Sahara 16

Chapter 5: How the Sahara Desert Formed 22

Chapter 6: The Extreme Weather of the Sahara...................28

Chapter 7: Water Sources in the Sahara Desert 34

Chapter 8: Nomadic Tribes of the Sahara 40

Chapter 9: The Great Sahara Desert Expeditions 46

Chapter 10: The Oases of the Sahara Desert......................52

Chapter 11: The Sahara's Mysterious Rock Art 58

Chapter 12: The Sahara's Role in Trade and Travel.........64

Chapter 13: Unique Plants of the Sahara Desert................69

Chapter 14: The Hidden Mountains of the Sahara.............75

Chapter 15: Camels: Ships of the Sahara Desert................81

Chapter 16: Life in the Sahara's Remote Villages.............87

Chapter 17: The Sahara's Impact on Global Climate.........93

Chapter 18: The Salt Trade Routes of the Sahara.............98

Chapter 19: Ancient Fossils in the Sahara Desert 103

Chapter 20: Modern Challenges Facing the Sahara Desert 108

Epilogue.. 114

Prologue

Welcome to the Sahara Desert! Imagine a place so vast, it's larger than many countries combined. The Sahara is the biggest hot desert on Earth, stretching across North Africa like a golden sea of sand. But it's not just endless dunes — the Sahara is full of amazing surprises. From ancient civilizations that once thrived here, to the plants and animals that call this harsh land home, the Sahara is a world full of wonder.

In this book, we'll take you on an exciting journey through the desert. You'll meet the brave people who have lived in the Sahara for thousands of years, discover how camels survive long treks in the heat, and learn about the secret oases that offer life in the middle of nowhere. We'll also explore the incredible fossils hidden beneath the sand, and even uncover how this desert helps shape our planet's climate.

So grab your hat and some sunscreen, because we're about to dive into the mysteries and magic of the Sahara Desert — a place unlike any other on Earth!

Chapter 1: The Origins of the Sahara Desert

The Sahara Desert, known as the world's largest hot desert, has a fascinating and complex history stretching back millions of years. To truly understand how this vast expanse of sand and rock came to be, we must travel far back in time to a period when the African continent looked very different from how it does today.

The origins of the Sahara Desert are rooted in the shifting climate patterns of Earth's history. Around 200 million years ago, during the time of the supercontinent Pangaea, the area that is now the Sahara was part of a lush, fertile region. It was home to rivers, lakes, and abundant plant and animal life. At that time, the landscape would have looked nothing like the barren, dry desert we know today. Instead, it was covered in forests and grasslands, with a climate much more like modern-day tropical or subtropical regions.

As the Earth's tectonic plates continued to move and shift, the landmasses that made up Pangaea began to break apart. Africa gradually drifted northward, and this movement played a significant role in shaping the climate of the continent. Over millions of years, as Africa moved closer to the equator, the region's climate began to change. The once-fertile lands started to dry out as the continent's position shifted. This process, known as desertification, occurred over thousands of years.

The Sahara's transformation into a desert was not a sudden event but rather a slow and gradual process influenced by several factors, including changes in Earth's orbit, volcanic activity, and global climate shifts. One of the key factors in the Sahara's formation is a phenomenon called the "Milankovitch cycles." These cycles refer to changes in Earth's position relative to the Sun over long periods. These variations affect the amount of sunlight that different parts of the Earth receive, which in turn influences global climate patterns. Around 5 to 10 million years ago, these cycles began to push the region that would become the Sahara into a more arid, desert-like climate.

Another crucial factor in the Sahara's formation was the uplift of the Atlas Mountains, located to the north of the desert. This geological event, which occurred around 65 million years ago, had a significant impact on the region's climate. The Atlas Mountains act as a barrier that blocks moist air from the Atlantic Ocean, preventing it from reaching the interior of the continent. As a result, the land to the south of the mountains, including the area that is now the Sahara, began to receive less rainfall. Over time, the lack of moisture led to the drying out of the land, further contributing to the desertification process.

The formation of the Sahara was not a simple, one-way transition from a green landscape to a desert. Throughout its history, the Sahara has undergone periods of change, alternating between wet and dry phases. One of the most significant of these wet periods occurred around 10,000 years ago during the African Humid Period. During this time, the Sahara was much wetter than it is today, with rivers, lakes, and even human settlements thriving in the region. Archaeological evidence suggests that early humans lived in the Sahara during this period, hunting animals like hippos and crocodiles and gathering plants from the fertile land.

The African Humid Period was caused by changes in Earth's orbit that brought more rainfall to the region. However, this wet phase did not last forever. Around 5,000 years ago, the climate began to shift once again, and the Sahara started to dry out. The lakes and rivers that had sustained life in the desert gradually disappeared, and the region became the arid, inhospitable environment we see today. This shift had a profound impact on the people and animals that lived in the Sahara, forcing them to migrate to more fertile areas to the south and along the Nile River.

Interestingly, the Sahara's desertification process is still ongoing. The desert continues to expand, encroaching on the surrounding savannah and grasslands. This phenomenon, known as desert expansion or desertification, is a major concern for the people who live in the region today. Human activities, such as overgrazing, deforestation, and poor land management, have accelerated the process, making the land even more vulnerable to becoming desert-like. Climate change is also playing a role, with rising temperatures and changing rainfall patterns contributing to the continued spread of the Sahara.

Despite its harsh, barren appearance today, the Sahara's history is a reminder of the dynamic nature of Earth's climate and landscapes. The desert that we see now is the result of millions of years of natural processes, shaped by the movement of continents, changes in Earth's orbit, and the rise and fall of mountains. It is a landscape that has been both wet and dry, green and barren, fertile and lifeless. While we may think of the Sahara as a permanent feature of the African continent, its history tells a different story—one of change, adaptation, and transformation over time.

The Sahara's origins also offer important lessons for understanding the broader forces that shape our planet. The same processes that created the desert millions of years ago—climate shifts, tectonic movements, and geological changes—are still at work today, influencing the landscapes and environments we see around the world. These forces remind us that Earth's surface is constantly changing, and that what may seem like a permanent feature, such as a desert or a mountain range, is in fact part of a much larger and ever-evolving system.

The desert's formation also serves as a testament to the resilience of life. Even in the most challenging environments, like the Sahara, life has found a way to adapt and survive. The plants and animals that live in the desert today have evolved remarkable strategies for coping with extreme heat and limited water. Similarly, human populations have long adapted to life in the Sahara, developing unique cultures and ways of living in harmony with their harsh surroundings.

In conclusion, the Sahara Desert's origins are deeply intertwined with the history of our planet. Its formation was the result of a complex interplay of natural forces, from tectonic movements and mountain building to changes in Earth's orbit and climate. What was once a lush, green landscape has, over millions of years, transformed into the vast desert we see today. Yet, even in its current form, the Sahara remains a dynamic and ever-changing environment, shaped by both natural processes and human activities. Its history is a reminder of the power of nature and the incredible ability of life to adapt to even the most extreme conditions.

Chapter 2: Wildlife in the Sahara's Sands

The Sahara Desert, despite its harsh and seemingly inhospitable environment, is home to a surprisingly diverse range of wildlife that has evolved to survive in one of the most extreme climates on Earth. Stretching across North Africa, the Sahara is not just an endless expanse of sand dunes. Its landscape includes rocky plateaus, gravel plains, dry valleys, and isolated oases, each offering different habitats that support unique forms of life. The animals that inhabit this vast desert have developed extraordinary adaptations to cope with extreme temperatures, limited water sources, and the relentless desert winds. From small insects to large mammals, and even some resilient plant species, the Sahara hosts a fascinating ecosystem that has learned to thrive in conditions that would be unbearable to most creatures.

The scorching daytime heat of the Sahara can reach temperatures over 120 degrees Fahrenheit (50 degrees Celsius), while nighttime temperatures can plummet to near freezing. Water is extremely scarce, with vast stretches of the desert going without any rainfall for years at a time. Yet, despite these formidable challenges, the Sahara is home to a variety of animal species, many of which have developed specialized behaviors and physical traits to conserve water and withstand the desert's heat.

One of the most iconic animals of the Sahara is the dromedary camel, often referred to as the "ship of the desert." These camels have long been domesticated by the people who live in the Sahara and are essential for survival in the harsh desert environment. Camels are uniquely suited to life in the desert. They can go for long periods without water—sometimes up to two weeks—because they are able to store fat in their humps, which can be metabolized for energy and hydration. Their thick fur protects them from the sun's intense heat, and their wide, padded feet allow them to walk easily on the loose sand without sinking. Additionally, camels have long eyelashes and closable nostrils to keep out the blowing sand, which can be fierce during desert storms. In many ways, camels are the perfect example of an animal perfectly adapted to the Sahara's challenges, and they remain a vital part of the lives of the desert's human inhabitants.

In addition to camels, the Sahara is home to a number of other large mammals, many of which are endangered due to habitat loss and human activities. The addax, for example, is a type of antelope that has evolved to live in some of the most arid parts of the desert. With its pale, sandy-colored coat, the addax blends in with the desert surroundings, offering it some protection from predators. Addaxes are highly adapted to life in the desert and can go for long periods without drinking water. They obtain most of the moisture they need from the plants they eat, which is a common adaptation among many desert herbivores. Unfortunately, the addax is critically endangered, with only a few hundred individuals remaining in the wild, largely due to overhunting and habitat destruction.

Another remarkable desert survivor is the fennec fox, a small nocturnal predator with oversized ears that help it dissipate heat and detect the movement of prey underground. The fennec fox has a light-colored coat that reflects the sun's rays during the day, and its thick fur also provides insulation during the cold desert nights. The fox's large ears are not just for cooling; they also enable the fennec fox to hear the slightest sounds, allowing it to locate small rodents, insects, and lizards, which make up the bulk of its diet. Fennec foxes are excellent diggers and often create burrows in the sand where they can escape the heat of the day, emerging at night when the desert cools down to hunt and scavenge.

Reptiles are another group of animals well represented in the Sahara, and they are particularly well-suited to desert life. The desert monitor lizard is one of the larger reptiles found in the Sahara, growing up to two meters in length. This lizard is an opportunistic predator, feeding on anything it can catch, including small mammals, birds, and insects. Like many desert animals, monitor lizards have adapted to survive in an environment where food is scarce and water is even scarcer. They are able to conserve water by excreting concentrated urine and reducing their activity during the hottest parts of the day. The desert monitor is also capable of storing fat in its tail, which can provide energy when food is hard to find.

The Saharan silver ant is another fascinating creature that has adapted to the extreme heat of the desert. These ants are known for their ability to withstand some of the highest temperatures of any terrestrial animal, often venturing out during the hottest part of the day when other creatures retreat to the shade. The silver ant's shiny, metallic exoskeleton helps reflect the sun's rays, keeping it cool as it scurries across the desert in search of food. These ants have a highly organized social structure, and they work together to bring food back to their nests, which are typically located underground where temperatures are cooler.

Birds, too, make their home in the Sahara, with many species migrating through the desert or living there year-round. The most famous of the Sahara's birds is probably the ostrich, a large, flightless bird that can be found in the more vegetated areas of the desert. Ostriches are well adapted to the harsh environment, with long legs that allow them to cover large distances in search of food and water. Their large eyes help them spot predators from far away, and they can run at speeds of up to 40 miles per hour (64 kilometers per hour) to escape danger. Ostriches have a varied diet that includes plants, seeds, and insects, and they are able to go without water for several days at a time, getting most of their moisture from the food they eat.

In addition to these larger birds, there are many smaller species that live in the Sahara, such as sandgrouse and larks. These birds are often specially adapted to the desert's conditions, with feathers that help them stay cool and behaviors that allow them to find food and water in an environment where both are scarce. Some birds, like the sandgrouse, have developed unique ways of gathering water. Male sandgrouse, for example, will fly long distances to water sources and then soak their belly feathers in the water. They will then return to their nests, where their chicks can drink the water from their feathers—a remarkable adaptation to the desert's challenges.

Insects and arachnids are also abundant in the Sahara. Scorpions, for instance, are common throughout the desert. The deathstalker scorpion, one of the most venomous scorpions in the world, can be found in the Sahara, and like many desert dwellers, it is nocturnal. By emerging at night, scorpions avoid the extreme heat of the day and can hunt for food in cooler temperatures. Scorpions rely on their venom to subdue prey, which usually consists of insects and other small animals. Their tough exoskeleton helps them retain moisture, a critical adaptation in such an arid environment.

Beetles are another important group of insects that have found ways to thrive in the Sahara. One species, the darkling beetle, has developed an ingenious method for collecting water. It stands on the tops of sand dunes early in the morning, where it can collect moisture from the air on its body. This moisture then condenses into droplets, which the beetle drinks—a vital survival strategy in a place where liquid water is almost nonexistent.

Oases, small fertile areas in the desert where water is present, serve as vital lifelines for many species in the Sahara. These areas, which may be fed by underground rivers or natural springs, are home to a greater variety of plants and animals than the surrounding desert. Date palms are often found growing in oases, and the presence of water attracts a range of wildlife, from migratory birds to small mammals. Oases provide essential resources for both animals and humans, and historically, they have been crucial stops for caravans traveling across the desert.

While life in the Sahara is tough, the desert's wildlife is a testament to the resilience and adaptability of nature. The animals that call the

Sahara home have evolved to survive in one of the most extreme environments on Earth. Their ability to find food, water, and shelter in such a harsh place demonstrates the incredible diversity of life that can flourish even in the most unlikely of places. From the majestic dromedary camel to the tiny but hardy Saharan silver ant, the creatures of the Sahara have carved out a niche in this seemingly barren landscape, turning the desert sands into a bustling, if hidden, ecosystem.

Chapter 3: The Sahara's Famous Sand Dunes

The Sahara Desert is perhaps best known for its iconic sand dunes, which stretch across vast portions of its landscape, creating a sea of rolling, golden hills that seem to go on forever. While much of the Sahara is made up of rocky plateaus, gravel plains, and rugged mountains, the sand dunes—known as "ergs" in Arabic—are the desert's most recognizable feature. These dunes are not just scenic wonders; they are constantly shifting, reshaping the landscape in response to the forces of wind and time. The Sahara's sand dunes have captivated the imaginations of explorers, artists, and travelers for centuries, representing both the beauty and the danger of the desert.

The formation of these dunes begins with the process of weathering, in which rocks and other materials are broken down into smaller particles by wind, water, and temperature changes. Over time, the rocks that once dominated the landscape are reduced to fine grains of sand. In areas where wind patterns are strong and consistent, these grains are swept up and carried across the desert. When the wind slows down, the sand is deposited, eventually accumulating to form the large dunes that dominate many areas of the Sahara.

One of the most striking features of the Sahara's sand dunes is their sheer size. Some of the dunes can reach towering heights of up to 180 meters (600 feet), making them among the tallest sand formations in the world. The Grand Erg Oriental, located in eastern Algeria, and the Grand Erg Occidental in the western part of the Sahara, are two of the largest sand seas in the desert, covering thousands of square kilometers. These vast expanses of sand are made up of countless individual dunes, each shaped and molded by the wind.

The shapes of the dunes vary greatly depending on the wind patterns and the type of sand that makes up the dunes. One of the most common dune shapes in the Sahara is the crescent-shaped barchan dune. Barchan dunes are formed by winds that blow consistently from one direction. As the wind pushes the sand, it creates a gentle slope on the windward side of the dune and a steeper slope on the leeward side. The result is a crescent-shaped dune with "horns" that point in the direction of the wind. Barchan dunes are highly mobile and can move across the desert at a rate of several meters per year, driven by the constant force of the wind.

In areas where the wind comes from multiple directions, different types of dunes can form. Star dunes, for example, are created when winds shift frequently, causing the sand to be pushed into different directions. These dunes have multiple arms radiating out from a central peak, giving them a star-like appearance. Star dunes tend to be more stable than barchan dunes, as the shifting winds prevent them from migrating as quickly.

Linear dunes, also known as seif dunes, are long, narrow dunes that can stretch for kilometers in straight or slightly curved lines. These dunes are formed by winds that blow from two different directions but are generally aligned in the same direction. Linear dunes can grow to impressive heights and are often found in areas where the sand supply is limited, as the wind tends to focus the available sand into these narrow ridges.

The size and shape of the dunes are not the only things that make them unique. The color of the sand itself can vary, depending on the minerals present in the surrounding rocks. While much of the sand in the Sahara is a golden or reddish hue, certain areas contain dunes that are white, pink, or even black. These color variations are the result of different mineral compositions in the rocks that were weathered to create the sand. For example, the reddish sand found in many parts of the Sahara contains high amounts of iron oxide, while the black sand found in some areas comes from volcanic rock.

Despite their beauty, the Sahara's sand dunes are also a symbol of the harshness and danger of the desert. The dunes are constantly shifting, and travelers who are unfamiliar with the landscape can easily become disoriented or lost. The relentless winds that shape the dunes can also whip up sandstorms, known locally as "khamsin" or "haboobs," which can obscure vision and make travel nearly impossible. These sandstorms are caused by strong winds blowing across the desert, lifting sand and dust into the air and creating a wall of moving particles that can stretch for miles. During a sandstorm, the sky turns an eerie yellow or reddish color, and visibility can be reduced to just a few meters. These storms can last for hours or even days, making them a serious hazard for anyone caught in their path.

Despite these dangers, the sand dunes of the Sahara have long been a source of fascination for both locals and visitors. The dunes play an important role in the culture and mythology of the desert's people. For centuries, the nomadic tribes of the Sahara, such as the Tuareg and the Berbers, have navigated the vast sea of sand using landmarks and ancient knowledge passed down through generations. To these people, the dunes are more than just a natural feature—they are a living, breathing part of the desert landscape.

The Tuareg, in particular, have developed a deep relationship with the dunes. Known as the "blue people" because of the indigo robes they wear, the Tuareg have lived in the Sahara for thousands of years, crossing the desert on camel caravans to trade goods such as salt, gold, and spices. The sand dunes, with their ever-changing forms, present a challenge to navigation, but the Tuareg have learned to read the subtle signs of the desert, such as the direction of the wind and the position of the stars, to find their way across the seemingly featureless landscape. To the Tuareg, the dunes are both a home and a barrier, a place of beauty and a source of hardship.

The dunes also play a significant role in the ecosystem of the Sahara. While the desert may seem barren at first glance, the sand dunes provide a habitat for a surprising number of plants and animals. Certain species of grasses and shrubs are able to take root in the sand, their deep roots helping to stabilize the dunes and prevent them from shifting too rapidly. These plants provide food and shelter for small animals, such as rodents, lizards, and insects, which in turn attract larger predators, like foxes and birds of prey. The dunes may seem lifeless, but they are actually teeming with life, much of it hidden beneath the surface of the sand.

One of the most remarkable features of the sand dunes is their ability to create "singing" or "booming" sounds. This phenomenon occurs when large amounts of sand slide down the face of a dune, creating vibrations that produce a low, humming sound. The exact cause of this sound is still not fully understood, but it is believed to be related to the movement of the sand particles and the way they rub against each other. The sound can be quite loud, sometimes reaching decibel levels comparable to a car engine, and it has been described as a deep, resonant hum that can be heard from miles away. These "singing" dunes have been a source of mystery and legend for centuries, with local people attributing the sounds to spirits or the voices of the desert itself.

Tourists are often drawn to the Sahara's sand dunes, particularly to the famous Erg Chebbi dunes in Morocco and the Erg Chigaga dunes in Algeria. These areas have become popular destinations for adventure seekers, who come to ride camels, go sandboarding, or simply marvel at the stunning beauty of the desert landscape. The experience of watching the sunrise or sunset over the dunes is often described as magical, with the changing light casting the sand in hues of gold, orange, and pink. Many travelers find that the vastness and solitude of the dunes provide a sense of peace and contemplation, as the quiet of the desert allows them to disconnect from the noise and distractions of modern life.

While the dunes are a major draw for tourists, they also pose challenges for the people who live in and around the Sahara. The shifting sands can bury roads, villages, and agricultural land, making life in the desert extremely difficult. In some areas, efforts have been made to stabilize the dunes by planting vegetation or building barriers to prevent the sand from encroaching on inhabited areas. However, the sheer size and power of the dunes make it difficult to control their movement, and the desert continues to reclaim land despite human efforts to resist it.

The sand dunes of the Sahara are a testament to the power of nature. They are constantly in motion, shaped by the wind into ever-changing forms that defy permanence. At the same time, they are symbols of both beauty and danger, offering a stark contrast to the harshness of the desert environment. For those who live in the Sahara, the dunes are both a challenge to be overcome and a source of inspiration, a reminder of the resilience and adaptability required to survive in one of the most extreme places on Earth.

In conclusion, the sand dunes of the Sahara Desert are much more than just piles of sand. They are the result of millions of years of geological and climatic processes, shaped by the forces of wind and erosion. They play an important role in the culture and mythology of the desert's people, and they are home to a surprising variety of plants and animals. The dunes are constantly shifting, creating a dynamic landscape that is both beautiful and dangerous. From the towering barchan dunes to the star-shaped sand formations, the dunes of the Sahara are a wonder of the natural world, a symbol of the desert's timeless and ever-changing nature.

Chapter 4: Ancient Civilizations of the Sahara

Long before the Sahara Desert became the vast, arid, and inhospitable expanse that we know today, it was a region that supported a number of thriving ancient civilizations. The Sahara, stretching across much of North Africa, has not always been a desert. For thousands of years, this region experienced periods of lush greenery, ample water, and flourishing ecosystems, making it a place where early human societies could develop and thrive. These ancient civilizations left behind remarkable evidence of their existence, from rock art and artifacts to early forms of agriculture and trade. Understanding the history of these early Saharan civilizations provides a window into how human beings adapted to environmental changes, built complex societies, and interacted with their surroundings over millennia.

Around 10,000 years ago, the Sahara was a vastly different place. During the early Holocene epoch, what is now a desert was once a landscape of lakes, rivers, grasslands, and forests. This period, known as the African Humid Period or the Green Sahara, was characterized by regular rainfall and a relatively mild climate, making the region suitable for human habitation. Archaeological evidence suggests that early human communities settled in this region, benefiting from the abundance of resources such as water, plants, and animals. These early Saharan peoples lived as hunter-gatherers, relying on fishing, hunting, and gathering wild plants for sustenance.

One of the most intriguing discoveries about these ancient civilizations comes from the rich rock art found throughout the Sahara, particularly in regions such as the Tassili n'Ajjer plateau in modern-day Algeria and the Tadrart Acacus in Libya. The rock art, which dates back thousands of years, provides a glimpse into the daily lives, beliefs, and environments of the people who lived there. These paintings and carvings depict scenes of hunting, fishing, herding, and even dancing, suggesting that the ancient inhabitants of the Sahara led vibrant and complex lives. The imagery also reveals a time when large animals, such as elephants, giraffes, and crocodiles, roamed the Sahara, indicating a much wetter and more fertile environment than the one we see today.

As the climate of the Sahara began to shift around 6,000 years ago, the region slowly started to dry out. This process, which took thousands of years, transformed the once-green Sahara into the desert it is today. However, even as the environment changed, the people of the Sahara adapted, developing new ways to survive in the increasingly arid landscape. One of the most significant developments during this period was the introduction of pastoralism—the herding of domesticated animals such as cattle, sheep, and goats. The ancient Saharans became skilled pastoralists, moving their herds across the landscape in search of water and grazing land. This shift from hunting and gathering to pastoralism represented a major transformation in their way of life, allowing them to continue thriving in a changing environment.

The introduction of pastoralism also led to the emergence of more permanent settlements, as communities established themselves near reliable water sources, such as oases, rivers, and lakes that remained in the desert even as other areas dried up. These early pastoralist societies began to develop more complex social structures, with evidence of trade, craftsmanship, and religious practices. The rock art of this period shows images of cattle, sheep, and goats, as well as the people who herded them, highlighting the central role that animals played in the lives of these ancient civilizations. In addition to herding, the people of the Sahara began to cultivate crops, such as millet and barley, in the wetter areas, marking the beginnings of agriculture in the region.

As the Sahara continued to dry out, the civilizations that once thrived there were forced to migrate or adapt even further. Some groups moved south, into the more fertile regions of the Sahel, while others remained in the Sahara, developing innovative ways to survive in the increasingly harsh environment. The Garamantes, an ancient Berber-speaking civilization that emerged in the Fezzan region of modern-day Libya, are one of the most remarkable examples of a society that managed to flourish in the desert. The Garamantes are believed to have emerged around 1,000 BCE and built a powerful kingdom that lasted for over a thousand years, reaching its peak between the 1st and 4th centuries CE.

The Garamantes are known for their advanced irrigation techniques, which allowed them to create a thriving agricultural society in the heart of the Sahara. They developed an intricate system of underground channels, known as "foggara," to tap into subterranean water sources. These channels, which extended for miles beneath the desert, brought water to the surface, enabling the Garamantes to irrigate their fields and grow crops such as wheat, barley, and dates. This system of irrigation was so effective that the Garamantes were able to support a population of tens of thousands, even in one of the most arid regions of the world.

The Garamantes also built a network of fortified towns and cities, some of which featured elaborate buildings, temples, and tombs. Archaeological excavations have uncovered the ruins of Garamantian settlements, revealing evidence of their sophisticated society. The capital of the Garamantian kingdom, Garama, was a bustling city with stone buildings, streets, and public spaces. The Garamantes were also skilled traders, playing a key role in the trans-Saharan trade routes that connected North Africa with sub-Saharan Africa. They traded goods such as gold, ivory, and slaves with their neighbors to the south, as well as with the Roman Empire to the north. The Garamantes' control of the trade routes allowed them to amass wealth and power, making them one of the most influential civilizations in the ancient Sahara.

Despite their achievements, the Garamantes eventually declined, possibly due to a combination of environmental changes, overuse of water resources, and pressure from external forces, including the expanding Roman Empire. By the 5th century CE, the Garamantian kingdom had largely collapsed, and its cities were abandoned. However, their legacy lives on in the ruins they left behind and in the continued use of some of their irrigation techniques by modern desert communities.

Another ancient civilization that thrived in the Sahara was the Kingdom of Kush, which was located to the southeast of the desert, in what is now Sudan. The Kingdom of Kush, which existed from around 1070 BCE to 350 CE, was centered along the Nile River and its tributaries, but its influence extended into the western reaches of the Sahara. The Kushites were known for their rich culture, monumental architecture, and powerful military. They built impressive pyramids, temples, and palaces, many of which still stand today in places like Meroë, the capital of the kingdom. The Kingdom of Kush was also deeply connected to Egypt, with the two civilizations engaging in both conflict and cooperation over the centuries. At times, the Kushites even ruled over Egypt, during the period known as the 25th Dynasty.

The Sahara played an important role in the trade networks of the Kingdom of Kush, as it provided a corridor for the movement of goods and people. The Kushites traded gold, ivory, and other valuable commodities with their neighbors to the north and west, and they maintained contacts with the Berber-speaking peoples of the desert. The Kingdom of Kush was also influenced by the cultures of the Sahara, as evidenced by the art, religion, and material culture of the region. The rise and fall of the Kingdom of Kush were shaped in part by the changing climate of the Sahara, as the desert expanded and contracted over the centuries.

The ancient civilizations of the Sahara were not limited to large kingdoms like the Garamantes and Kushites. Many smaller, less well-known societies also flourished in the desert, each adapting to the unique challenges of their environment. One such group was the

Bantu-speaking peoples who lived in the western Sahara and Sahel regions during the early Holocene. These communities engaged in fishing, hunting, and gathering, as well as early forms of agriculture. Their pottery, tools, and burial practices provide valuable insights into the lives of these ancient people.

Additionally, the Tuareg, a nomadic Berber-speaking people, have long inhabited the central Sahara. While the Tuareg are still present in the region today, their ancestors have been traveling the desert for thousands of years. The Tuareg developed a deep understanding of the desert's ecology and geography, which allowed them to navigate its vast expanses and survive in one of the harshest environments on Earth. The Tuareg were also skilled traders, guiding caravans across the desert along ancient trade routes, transporting goods such as salt, gold, and slaves. The Tuareg's unique culture, language, and traditions have been passed down through generations, preserving a connection to the ancient civilizations that once thrived in the Sahara.

The Sahara has always been a region of great diversity, both in terms of its people and its environment. While today it is often seen as a barren wasteland, the Sahara was once home to some of the most advanced and complex civilizations of the ancient world. These societies were able to adapt to the changing climate, developing innovative technologies and social structures that allowed them to thrive in a region that most would consider uninhabitable. From the hunter-gatherers of the Green Sahara to the powerful kingdoms of the Garamantes and Kush, the ancient civilizations of the Sahara left an indelible mark on the history of Africa and the world.

The story of the ancient civilizations of the Sahara is a testament to the resilience and ingenuity of human beings. Even in the face of environmental challenges, these early societies found ways to adapt and flourish, creating rich cultures and lasting legacies. Today, the ruins, rock art, and artifacts they left behind offer us a glimpse into a world that once existed in what is now the world's largest hot desert. Their story is a reminder that the Sahara, while harsh and unforgiving, was once a land of life, culture, and civilization.

Chapter 5: How the Sahara Desert Formed

The formation of the Sahara Desert, the largest hot desert in the world, is a fascinating story that spans millions of years and involves complex geological, climatic, and environmental processes. Today, the Sahara is a vast, arid expanse stretching across much of northern Africa, covering approximately 9 million square kilometers. It is known for its extreme temperatures, towering sand dunes, and sparse vegetation. However, the Sahara has not always been a desert, and its transformation into the dry, barren landscape we see today is the result of a long history of natural change. Understanding how the Sahara Desert formed requires an exploration of ancient geological shifts, climate cycles, and the ever-changing relationship between the Earth's atmosphere and surface.

To comprehend how the Sahara became the desert it is today, it is essential to look back hundreds of millions of years to the time when the African continent was part of the ancient supercontinent Gondwana. Around 300 million years ago, during the late Carboniferous and early Permian periods, Gondwana was situated near the South Pole. At this time, much of what is now the Sahara was covered by glaciers and ice sheets as the Earth was experiencing an ice age. This icy environment was in stark contrast to the Sahara's current climate. Over millions of years, as the supercontinent Gondwana began to break apart, the landmass that would eventually become Africa drifted northward.

As the African continent moved closer to the equator during the Mesozoic era (between 252 and 66 million years ago), the region that is now the Sahara experienced a series of significant geological and climatic changes. During much of this time, the Sahara was part of a vast, shallow sea known as the Tethys Sea, which stretched across what is now North Africa and into parts of Europe and Asia. This ancient sea was home to a rich array of marine life, including ammonites, fish, and other marine organisms, some of whose fossilized remains can still be found in the desert today.

The Tethys Sea eventually began to recede as tectonic forces caused the African and Eurasian plates to converge. This collision of tectonic plates gave rise to the formation of the Atlas Mountains in northwestern Africa and the Mediterranean Sea. As the sea retreated, much of the Sahara became a coastal plain, and over time, layers of sediment deposited by rivers and ancient marine environments built up across the region. The shifting of tectonic plates also caused volcanic activity in the area, leading to the creation of volcanic mountains and plateaus that are still visible in parts of the Sahara today, such as the Ahaggar Mountains in Algeria and the Tibesti Mountains in Chad.

Around 65 million years ago, as the dinosaurs were going extinct and the Earth entered the Cenozoic era, the region that is now the Sahara began to experience periods of desertification. However, the transformation from a lush, green environment to a full-fledged desert was not linear. Instead, the climate of the Sahara has fluctuated dramatically over millions of years due to natural variations in the Earth's orbit, axis tilt, and atmospheric conditions. These fluctuations have led to alternating periods of wet and dry climates, shaping the Sahara into its current form.

One of the most important factors in the formation of the Sahara Desert is the Earth's orbit and its effect on the climate of northern Africa. The Earth's orbit around the Sun is not a perfect circle; it is slightly elliptical, and the shape of this ellipse changes over time in cycles known as Milankovitch cycles. These cycles, which occur over tens of thousands to hundreds of thousands of years, influence the amount of solar radiation that different parts of the Earth receive, affecting global climate patterns. In particular, the tilt of the Earth's axis, which varies between 22.1 and 24.5 degrees, plays a crucial role in determining the strength of the monsoon rains that occur in tropical and subtropical regions.

During periods when the Earth's axis is tilted more sharply (closer to 24.5 degrees), northern Africa receives more intense summer sunlight, which strengthens the African monsoon. This monsoon brings heavy rainfall to the Sahara, transforming the region into a green and fertile landscape. During these "Green Sahara" periods, large lakes, rivers, and wetlands formed across the desert, supporting abundant plant and animal life. Archaeological evidence shows that during these wet periods, early human populations flourished in the Sahara, hunting, fishing, and herding animals in what was then a verdant savannah.

One of the most recent and well-known Green Sahara periods occurred between 10,000 and 5,000 years ago, during the early Holocene epoch. This period, often referred to as the African Humid Period, saw the Sahara covered with grasslands, savannas, and forests, and it was home to numerous species of animals, including elephants, giraffes, and hippos. The early human civilizations that inhabited the Sahara during this time left behind rock art, tools, and other artifacts that provide insight into their way of life. These ancient peoples lived near large lakes and rivers, such as Lake Mega-Chad, which was one of the largest freshwater lakes in the world at the time.

However, the African Humid Period did not last indefinitely. As the Earth's axis tilt gradually shifted and the amount of solar radiation in the region decreased, the monsoon rains weakened. Over the course of several thousand years, the Sahara began to dry out, and the lakes, rivers, and grasslands gradually gave way to sand dunes, gravel plains, and rocky plateaus. This process of desertification was slow but relentless, and by around 5,000 years ago, the Sahara had become the arid desert we see today. The people who had lived in the Sahara during the Green Sahara period were forced to migrate, with many moving southward to the more fertile regions of the Sahel and the Nile Valley.

While the shift from a Green Sahara to a desert was largely driven by natural climate cycles, other factors also played a role in the desertification process. For example, changes in vegetation cover and the Earth's albedo (the reflection of sunlight from the surface) may have contributed to the drying of the region. As the vegetation that once covered the Sahara disappeared, the land became more reflective, which in turn caused the region to absorb less heat from the Sun. This feedback loop may have further weakened the monsoon rains, accelerating the desertification process.

The Sahara Desert as we know it today is not a uniform expanse of sand dunes; in fact, sand dunes (known as "ergs") only cover about 20% of the Sahara's surface. The majority of the desert consists of rocky plateaus, gravel plains, and mountains. These different landscapes are the result of various geological processes, including erosion, volcanic activity, and tectonic movements. Wind and water have also played a significant role in shaping the Sahara, carving out deep valleys, creating vast salt flats, and forming the sand dunes that are so iconic of the desert.

The desertification of the Sahara has had a profound impact on the region's ecosystems and human populations. As the climate became increasingly arid, many plant and animal species that had once thrived in the Green Sahara were forced to either adapt to the harsh desert conditions or migrate to more hospitable environments. Today, the Sahara is home to only a limited number of species, including desert-adapted plants such as cacti and acacia trees, as well as animals like camels, desert foxes, and scorpions. The extreme temperatures and lack of water in the desert make it difficult for most forms of life to survive.

Human populations have also had to adapt to the challenges of life in the Sahara. Nomadic tribes, such as the Tuareg and the Berbers, have developed ways of living in harmony with the desert, relying on camels for transportation and moving between oases to find water and grazing land for their livestock. For centuries, these desert peoples have played a crucial role in the trans-Saharan trade routes, transporting goods such as gold, salt, and spices across the desert. The Tuareg, in particular, have become known as the "blue people" of the Sahara, due to the indigo-dyed clothing they wear to protect themselves from the sun.

The Sahara continues to evolve, as climate and environmental conditions change over time. While it is currently one of the driest places on Earth, the Sahara has not reached a state of permanent aridity. Some scientists predict that future changes in the Earth's orbit could lead to another Green Sahara period, with monsoon rains returning to the region and transforming it once again into a fertile landscape. These climate cycles are part of the natural ebb and flow of the Earth's climate system, and they remind us that even seemingly unchanging environments like the Sahara are constantly in flux.

In recent years, human activities such as deforestation, overgrazing, and climate change have also contributed to the expansion of deserts, a process known as desertification. The Sahara has expanded southward into the Sahel region, displacing communities and reducing the availability of arable land. Efforts are being made to combat desertification through initiatives such as the Great Green Wall project, which aims to plant trees and restore vegetation across the Sahel to slow the spread of the desert.

In conclusion, the Sahara Desert's formation is the result of millions of years of geological and climatic changes. From its origins as part of the ancient Tethys Sea to its transformation into a fertile savannah and eventually into the arid desert we know today, the Sahara's history is one of constant change and adaptation. While the desert may seem like a timeless and unchanging landscape, it is, in fact, a dynamic and ever-evolving environment. The forces that shaped the Sahara in the past, including tectonic movements, climate cycles, and environmental feedback loops, continue to influence the region today, and they will play a role in determining its future. Whether the Sahara will remain a desert or one day return to its former green state remains to be seen, but its history provides a fascinating glimpse into the complex interplay between the Earth's natural systems.

27

Chapter 6: The Extreme Weather of the Sahara

The Sahara Desert, the largest hot desert in the world, is known for its extreme weather conditions. Covering roughly 9 million square kilometers across North Africa, the Sahara is a place of dramatic contrasts. It is often considered one of the harshest environments on Earth, characterized by blistering heat during the day, frigid temperatures at night, and very little rainfall. The combination of these factors creates a challenging climate that has shaped the landscape, the plant and animal life, and the people who inhabit the region. Understanding the extreme weather of the Sahara requires a close look at its unique atmospheric patterns, temperature fluctuations, wind systems, and precipitation, as well as the long-term impacts of climate change on the region.

One of the most striking features of the Sahara's climate is its extremely high daytime temperatures. During the summer months, it is not uncommon for the temperature to soar well above 40°C (104°F), with some areas reaching as high as 50°C (122°F). The highest temperature ever recorded in the Sahara was 58°C (136.4°F) in Aziziyah, Libya, in 1922, though this record has been disputed. Regardless, temperatures in the desert routinely rank among the highest on the planet, making it a place of intense heat.

The high temperatures in the Sahara are due in large part to its location within the subtropical high-pressure zone, also known as the horse latitudes. This zone is found between 20° and 30° north of the equator, where descending air from the upper atmosphere creates a belt of dry, stable air. This descending air warms as it compresses, and the lack of clouds allows the sun's intense rays to beat down directly on the desert surface. As a result, the Sahara experiences some of the highest solar radiation levels in the world. The clear skies and lack of moisture in the air mean that there is little to absorb or reflect the sun's heat, allowing the desert floor to heat up rapidly.

However, the extreme heat of the Sahara is only part of the story. One of the most surprising aspects of the desert's weather is the dramatic drop in temperature that occurs at night. Despite the scorching heat of the day, nighttime temperatures in the Sahara can plummet to near freezing, especially during the winter months. It is not uncommon for the temperature to drop by as much as 20°C (36°F) or more between day and night, creating a phenomenon known as diurnal temperature variation. In some parts of the desert, temperatures can fall below 0°C (32°F) at night, particularly in the higher elevations and during the colder months.

The reason for this extreme temperature swing is the same factor that causes the intense heat during the day—the lack of moisture in the air. In humid environments, water vapor in the atmosphere helps to trap heat, keeping temperatures relatively stable between day and night. In the Sahara, however, the air is extremely dry, meaning there is little water vapor to retain the heat from the sun. As soon as the sun sets, the desert loses heat rapidly through radiation, and without clouds or moisture to hold onto that heat, the temperature drops dramatically.

This stark contrast between day and night temperatures can have a significant impact on the people, animals, and plants that live in the desert. Human inhabitants must dress in layers to protect themselves from the extreme heat during the day and the cold at night. Many animals that call the Sahara home have adapted to the temperature fluctuations by being nocturnal, seeking shelter from the heat during the day and becoming active only after the sun has set. Likewise, desert plants have developed specialized strategies to conserve water and survive the wide temperature swings.

In addition to extreme temperatures, the Sahara is also known for its powerful wind systems. The desert is regularly buffeted by strong winds, which play a major role in shaping its landscape. One of the most well-known winds in the Sahara is the harmattan, a dry and dusty trade wind that blows from the northeast across the desert during the winter months. The harmattan wind originates over the Sahara and blows toward the Atlantic Ocean, carrying with it fine particles of sand and dust. These dust storms can be so intense that they obscure visibility and create hazardous conditions for travelers. The harmattan is often called the "doctor wind" because, despite its drying effects, it is believed to have some health benefits, such as clearing the air of harmful pathogens.

Another significant wind in the Sahara is the sirocco, a hot, dry wind that blows from the Sahara northward into Europe, particularly affecting countries like Italy, Spain, and Greece. The sirocco is sometimes referred to as the "desert wind" because it originates in the desert and can carry dust and sand across the Mediterranean Sea. In addition to its heat, the sirocco is known for causing rapid temperature increases and creating oppressive conditions in the regions it affects. In some cases, the sirocco can cause temperatures in southern Europe to spike by as much as 20°C (36°F) in just a few hours.

Wind plays a crucial role in the formation of the Sahara's famous sand dunes, or "ergs," which cover roughly 20% of the desert's surface. These massive sand dunes, some of which can reach heights of over 180 meters (590 feet), are constantly shifting as the wind moves the sand from one place to another. The process of wind erosion, known as deflation, scours the desert floor, removing fine particles of sand and dust and leaving behind the larger, heavier particles. Over time, the wind's action shapes the dunes into a variety of forms, including crescent-shaped barchan dunes, linear dunes, and star dunes. The constant movement of the sand gives the Sahara a dynamic, ever-changing landscape.

In addition to the harmattan and sirocco winds, the Sahara occasionally experiences violent dust storms, known as "haboobs." These storms occur when a sudden downdraft of air, typically caused by a thunderstorm, hits the desert floor and kicks up large amounts of sand and dust. Haboobs can form towering walls of dust that stretch for kilometers, and they move quickly across the desert, engulfing everything in their path. These dust storms can reduce visibility to near zero, making travel extremely dangerous, and they can carry dust particles thousands of kilometers, even reaching the Americas. The dust from the Sahara is rich in nutrients, and when it is blown across the Atlantic Ocean, it helps to fertilize the Amazon rainforest.

Despite the Sahara's reputation for being bone-dry, rainfall does occur in some parts of the desert, albeit infrequently. The Sahara is classified as a hyper-arid region, meaning that it receives less than 25 millimeters (1 inch) of rainfall per year on average. Some areas of the desert, particularly in the central and eastern regions, may go years without any measurable rainfall. When rain does fall, it is often in the form of short, intense thunderstorms that can cause flash floods. Because the desert soil is hard and compacted, it does not absorb water easily, so when rain does come, it tends to run off quickly, creating temporary rivers and lakes.

The western Sahara, near the Atlantic coast, receives slightly more rainfall than the interior of the desert, due to the influence of the Atlantic Ocean. Coastal areas may experience fog and dew, which can provide a small but important source of moisture for plants and animals. In some parts of the desert, particularly near mountain ranges and high plateaus, occasional rainfall can create oases, where underground water sources come to the surface, allowing plants to grow and providing a vital source of water for both humans and wildlife.

While rain is rare in the Sahara, the desert is not entirely devoid of life-giving water. Many parts of the Sahara are underlain by vast aquifers—underground reservoirs of water that were deposited during earlier, wetter periods in the Earth's history. These aquifers, some of which are ancient and non-renewable, provide water to oases and desert communities through wells and irrigation systems. The presence of these underground water sources has made it possible for people to live in the Sahara for thousands of years, despite the harsh and arid conditions.

In recent years, the Sahara's climate has become an area of particular interest to scientists studying climate change. The Sahara is highly sensitive to changes in global climate patterns, and there is evidence that the desert is expanding southward into the Sahel region—a process known as desertification. Human activities, such as deforestation, overgrazing, and poor land management, have exacerbated this problem by reducing vegetation cover and increasing soil erosion. Climate change, which is leading to higher temperatures and more erratic rainfall patterns, is likely to intensify these trends, making life in and around the Sahara even more challenging.

One of the most significant climate changes that the Sahara has experienced in the past is the alternation between wet and dry periods. During the African Humid Period, which occurred between 10,000 and 5,000 years ago, the Sahara was a lush, green landscape, with large lakes, rivers, and abundant plant and animal life. This period of increased rainfall was driven by changes in the Earth's orbit and axial tilt, which intensified the African monsoon. As the Earth's orbit shifted, the monsoon weakened, and the Sahara gradually dried out, becoming the desert we see today. Some scientists believe that future changes in the Earth's orbit could eventually bring about another wet period in the Sahara, though this is likely to be thousands of years away.

In addition to natural climate variability, human-induced climate change is likely to have significant impacts on the Sahara in the coming decades. Rising global temperatures are expected to increase the frequency and intensity of heatwaves in the desert, making it even more inhospitable for both humans and wildlife. At the same time, changing rainfall patterns could lead to more extreme weather events, such as flash floods and dust storms. These changes will have profound implications for the people who live in and around the Sahara, many of whom rely on agriculture and livestock herding to survive.

In conclusion, the extreme weather of the Sahara Desert is the result of a complex interplay between atmospheric conditions, geographical location, and climate variability. The desert's scorching daytime heat, freezing nighttime temperatures, powerful winds, and scarce rainfall make it one of the most hostile environments on Earth. Yet, despite these harsh conditions, the Sahara is a dynamic and ever-changing landscape, shaped by the forces of nature over millions of years. As climate change continues to alter weather patterns around the globe, the Sahara may experience even more extreme weather in the future, further challenging the plants, animals, and people who call this vast desert home.

Chapter 7: Water Sources in the Sahara Desert

Water sources in the Sahara Desert are among the most precious and crucial resources in one of the world's driest and harshest environments. The Sahara, which spans approximately 9 million square kilometers across North Africa, is often associated with arid landscapes, scorching heat, and vast expanses of sand dunes, but beneath its surface and in hidden pockets of its terrain, there are vital water sources that support life in this extreme desert. Water is a critical element for both human populations and the diverse array of wildlife that have adapted to the Sahara's harsh conditions. These water sources, though rare and often elusive, have sustained civilizations, trade routes, and ecosystems for thousands of years. Understanding where water can be found in the Sahara, how it is accessed, and how it is used is key to appreciating how life continues to thrive in such a challenging environment.

One of the primary water sources in the Sahara Desert is underground aquifers. These aquifers are large, underground reservoirs of water that have accumulated over thousands, and in some cases millions, of years. During past geological epochs, the Sahara was not always the vast desert it is today. There were periods, such as the African Humid Period (between 10,000 and 5,000 years ago), when the region was lush with vegetation, rivers, and lakes. During these wetter periods, water percolated through the soil and became trapped in underground layers of rock and sediment, forming aquifers. These ancient water reserves, often called "fossil water," are a finite resource because they were replenished during wetter climatic periods that no longer occur on the same scale today.

Aquifers in the Sahara can be vast, covering thousands of square kilometers and containing billions of cubic meters of water. Some of the most significant aquifers in the Sahara include the Nubian

Sandstone Aquifer System, which lies beneath parts of Chad, Libya, Egypt, and Sudan, and the North Western Sahara Aquifer System, which extends under Algeria, Tunisia, and Libya. These aquifers are often located deep beneath the surface, sometimes hundreds of meters below ground. To access this water, people have developed wells and other systems for extracting water from the aquifers, often using traditional methods like hand-dug wells or more modern techniques such as motorized pumps.

In many cases, the water from these aquifers reaches the surface naturally, creating oases. Oases are some of the most famous and iconic water sources in the Sahara, serving as vital lifelines for both human and animal life. An oasis is typically a fertile area in the desert where water from an underground source comes to the surface, often through springs or shallow wells. The presence of water allows for the growth of vegetation, including date palms, grasses, and other plants that can survive in the harsh desert climate. These plants, in turn, provide food and shelter for animals and serve as critical resources for human populations.

Oases have been central to the development of human settlements and trade routes in the Sahara for thousands of years. Some of the most well-known oases include the Siwa Oasis in Egypt, the Kufra Oasis in Libya, and the Tafilalt Oasis in Morocco. These oases have supported agriculture, providing water for crops such as dates, wheat, and barley. Date palms, in particular, are a crucial crop in the Sahara, as they can survive in extremely arid conditions and provide a valuable source of nutrition. In addition to agriculture, oases have long been important stops for caravans and traders traveling across the Sahara, providing essential water and rest for both people and animals.

The strategic location of oases along ancient trade routes, such as the Trans-Saharan trade routes, made them critical hubs for commerce and cultural exchange. For centuries, camel caravans would traverse the vast desert, carrying goods such as salt, gold, ivory, and spices across the Sahara, with oases serving as essential waypoints. These trade routes helped connect sub-Saharan Africa with the Mediterranean world, and oases played a pivotal role in facilitating the movement of goods and people. The presence of water in these otherwise inhospitable landscapes was often the difference between life and death for travelers, making oases indispensable to the survival of both trade and desert communities.

In addition to oases and aquifers, the Sahara also contains seasonal rivers, known as wadis, which can serve as temporary sources of water. Wadis are dry riverbeds that only fill with water during rare and often short-lived rainstorms. Because rain is so infrequent in the Sahara, with some areas receiving less than 25 millimeters (1 inch) of rainfall per year, wadis are typically dry for most of the year. However, when rain does fall, it can be intense and lead to flash floods, causing wadis to fill rapidly with water. These temporary rivers provide a crucial source of water for the surrounding environment, allowing plants to bloom and animals to drink.

Wadis are often located in more mountainous regions of the Sahara, where elevation can lead to slightly more rainfall and runoff. For example, the Ahaggar Mountains in Algeria and the Tibesti Mountains in Chad are home to wadis that fill with water after rare storms. Though these rivers are short-lived, the water they provide can be stored in natural depressions or collected by people living in the area. Wadis also contribute to the formation of temporary lakes and ponds, which provide a habitat for migratory birds and other wildlife during the brief periods when water is available.

In some cases, larger lakes have existed in the Sahara in the past, although many of them have since dried up or shrunk considerably. One of the most significant examples is Lake Mega-Chad, which, during its peak about 7,000 years ago, was one of the largest freshwater lakes in the world, covering an area of more than 400,000 square kilometers. Today, only remnants of this massive lake remain, most notably Lake Chad, which is a fraction of its former size and is rapidly shrinking due to climate change, overuse, and desertification. Nevertheless, Lake Chad continues to be an important water source for millions of people living in the surrounding region.

The Sahara is also home to several smaller, more ephemeral lakes, which appear during rare rainy seasons. These lakes may form in natural basins or depressions in the desert, where rainfall accumulates and creates temporary bodies of water. These ephemeral lakes often evaporate quickly under the hot desert sun, but while they exist, they provide a vital source of water for wildlife, such as birds, amphibians, and even some fish species. In fact, some species of fish in the Sahara have adapted to these temporary conditions, entering a state of dormancy during dry periods and becoming active again when water returns.

Although rainfall is rare in the Sahara, certain areas of the desert experience more consistent precipitation than others. The northern fringes of the desert, near the Mediterranean coast, and the western edges along the Atlantic Ocean receive slightly more rainfall due to the influence of coastal weather patterns. In these areas, moisture from the sea can lead to occasional rain or fog, which provides a small but important source of water. For example, the coastal region of Mauritania receives occasional fog, which helps sustain small populations of plants and animals that have adapted to the desert environment. Similarly, the Tibesti Mountains and other highland areas in the Sahara can experience more rainfall than the surrounding desert, making them key locations for accessing water.

Another fascinating method by which water is obtained in the Sahara is through the collection of dew and condensation. In the driest parts of the desert, where rainfall is almost nonexistent, dew can form in the early morning when the temperature drops, and moisture in the air condenses on the surface of rocks, plants, or even specially designed structures. Some desert plants have evolved to capture and channel dew toward their roots, providing them with a small but vital source of water. Similarly, some human communities have developed traditional methods for collecting condensation, using materials like cloth or specialized metal structures that can trap moisture from the air during the cool nighttime hours.

Human ingenuity has long been a key factor in accessing and managing water sources in the Sahara. Traditional methods of water management, such as the foggara system, have been developed over centuries to make the most of limited water resources. The foggara, also known as qanat, is an ancient underground irrigation system that was developed in regions of the Sahara, particularly in Algeria and Libya. The system involves digging a series of underground tunnels that connect wells to agricultural fields or settlements. The tunnels are designed to channel water from an underground aquifer to the surface in a controlled and sustainable manner, minimizing evaporation and ensuring that the water is available for crops and human use.

The foggara system is an ingenious solution to the problem of water scarcity in the desert, allowing communities to farm and live in areas where surface water is almost nonexistent. The system also demonstrates the importance of careful water management in a region where overuse or mismanagement of water resources can have devastating consequences. In recent years, concerns have grown about the sustainability of water extraction from the Sahara's aquifers. While modern technology, such as motorized pumps and large-scale irrigation systems, has made it easier to access underground water, it has also led to over-extraction in some areas, depleting aquifers that are not easily replenished. As climate change and desertification continue to affect the region, the pressure on these limited water sources is likely to increase.

In conclusion, water sources in the Sahara Desert, though scarce and difficult to access, are the lifeblood of this vast and extreme environment. From ancient aquifers and hidden oases to ephemeral wadis and lakes, water in the Sahara is found in a variety of forms, each playing a crucial role in supporting the people, animals, and plants that call the desert home. The ingenuity and resourcefulness of human populations in the Sahara have enabled them to survive and even thrive in one of the most inhospitable places on Earth, thanks to their ability to harness and manage these precious water sources. As climate change and human activities continue to reshape the landscape of the Sahara, the future of its water resources remains uncertain, but their importance cannot be overstated in sustaining life in this vast and ancient desert.

Chapter 8: Nomadic Tribes of the Sahara

The nomadic tribes of the Sahara Desert are a fascinating subject, representing a way of life that has persisted for thousands of years, despite the harsh conditions and the changing world around them. These tribes, including the Tuareg, Bedouin, Tubu, and others, have developed intricate cultures, survival strategies, and social systems that allow them to thrive in one of the world's most extreme environments. Life in the Sahara is characterized by extreme heat, scarce water, vast distances, and an ever-changing landscape of sand dunes and rocky plateaus. Yet, despite these challenges, the nomadic tribes have adapted to live in harmony with the desert, moving across its vast expanses in search of resources, trading goods, and maintaining their traditional customs and way of life.

One of the most well-known and prominent nomadic groups in the Sahara is the Tuareg. The Tuareg people are often referred to as the "blue people" due to the indigo-dyed cloth that they wear, which stains their skin blue. The Tuareg are part of the Berber ethnic group, and their traditional homelands span across the central Sahara, including parts of modern-day Niger, Mali, Algeria, Libya, and Burkina Faso. For centuries, the Tuareg have been expert traders and guides, leading caravans across the vast desert on camels, which they call the "ships of the desert." The Tuareg's deep knowledge of the desert's geography, weather patterns, and oases has allowed them to survive and thrive in one of the most unforgiving environments on Earth.

Traditionally, the Tuareg were semi-nomadic, combining trade with seasonal migrations to find pasture for their livestock, particularly goats, sheep, and camels. The Tuareg social structure is organized into clans, and they have a long history of matrilineal inheritance, which means that property and lineage are passed down through the female line. Women in Tuareg society traditionally have a relatively high status compared to other nomadic cultures, and they play important roles in decision-making, family life, and cultural traditions. Tuareg men, on the other hand, are often responsible for leading caravans, protecting the tribe, and herding livestock. One of the most distinctive features of Tuareg men is their tradition of wearing veils, known as *tagelmust*, which cover their faces and protect them from the harsh desert winds and sand.

The Tuareg's mastery of the camel has been central to their ability to traverse the Sahara. Camels are ideally suited to desert life, as they can go for long periods without water, withstand the extreme heat, and carry heavy loads across vast distances. The Tuareg used camels not only for transportation but also as a symbol of wealth and status. The camels were critical for their role in the trans-Saharan trade routes that connected North Africa, the Sahel, and sub-Saharan Africa. Goods such as salt, gold, ivory, spices, and slaves were transported across the desert in long camel caravans, often guided by Tuareg nomads. The salt trade, in particular, was vital, as salt was a precious commodity in both African and European markets. The Tuareg's role as traders helped them accumulate wealth and influence, even as they maintained their nomadic lifestyle.

Another major nomadic group in the Sahara is the Bedouin, a term that broadly refers to nomadic Arab tribes who traditionally inhabited the deserts of North Africa and the Middle East. The Bedouin lifestyle revolves around herding livestock, particularly camels, goats, and sheep, and moving seasonally in search of grazing lands and water sources. The Bedouin are known for their strong sense of hospitality, tribal loyalty, and adherence to traditional customs, which are deeply rooted in their Islamic faith. Bedouin society is organized around extended families and clans, and social relationships are governed by strict codes of honor and mutual respect.

Historically, the Bedouin tribes were not confined to the Sahara but also ranged across the Arabian Peninsula, the Sinai Desert, and the Syrian Desert. In the Sahara, Bedouin tribes can be found in regions such as the Western Sahara, Mauritania, and parts of Egypt and Libya. Like the Tuareg, the Bedouin have long been skilled desert navigators and traders, and their nomadic lifestyle allowed them to adapt to the ever-changing desert environment. While modern technology and political changes have led many Bedouin to settle in towns and cities, there are still groups who continue to live as nomads, maintaining their traditional way of life.

The Tubu, another important nomadic group in the Sahara, inhabit regions of northern Chad, southern Libya, and eastern Niger. The Tubu are divided into two main subgroups: the Teda, who live primarily in the Tibesti Mountains, and the Daza, who live in the more arid plains and deserts to the south. The Tubu are renowned for their endurance and resilience in the face of the Sahara's extreme conditions. They are expert herders, hunters, and traders, and like the Tuareg and Bedouin, they rely heavily on camels for transportation across the desert.

The Tubu's homeland in the Tibesti Mountains is one of the most remote and rugged regions of the Sahara. The mountains provide a relatively cooler climate and more abundant water sources than the surrounding desert, allowing the Tubu to raise livestock and cultivate crops such as millet and dates in small oases. However, life in the Tibesti Mountains is far from easy, and the Tubu have developed a strong sense of independence and self-reliance. They are known for their skill in navigating the rocky terrain and their ability to survive in areas with minimal water and vegetation. The Tubu have historically been involved in trade and raiding, and they have a long tradition of resisting external control, whether from colonial powers or modern governments.

In addition to these larger nomadic groups, there are numerous smaller tribes and communities that continue to live a nomadic or semi-nomadic lifestyle in the Sahara. These groups often have distinct cultural practices, languages, and survival strategies that are adapted to the specific regions they inhabit. For example, the Sahrawi people, who live in the Western Sahara and parts of Mauritania and Algeria, are descendants of Arab-Berber tribes and have a long history of nomadism, trade, and conflict in the desert. Similarly, the Moorish people of Mauritania, who are of mixed Arab and Berber descent, traditionally lived as nomads, moving with their herds across the desert in search of pasture and water.

The survival of nomadic tribes in the Sahara is largely dependent on their ability to find and manage water resources, which are incredibly scarce in the desert. Nomads rely on oases, wells, and underground aquifers for water, and they have developed intricate systems for locating and preserving water. The ability to read the desert landscape, including the location of wadis (seasonal rivers), underground springs, and vegetation that indicates the presence of water, is a critical skill for nomadic tribes. Water is not only essential for drinking but also for sustaining livestock, which are the primary source of food, transportation, and trade for many nomadic groups.

Livestock plays a central role in the nomadic lifestyle, providing food, clothing, and materials for shelter. Camels, goats, and sheep are the most common animals herded by nomadic tribes in the Sahara. Camels, in particular, are prized for their ability to survive long periods without water, carry heavy loads, and provide milk, meat, and hides. Goat and sheep herding is also important, as these animals provide milk, meat, and wool, which can be used for clothing and blankets or traded for other goods. The nomadic lifestyle is highly dependent on the health and well-being of livestock, and nomads must constantly move to find new grazing areas and avoid overgrazing the land.

Despite the nomadic way of life being deeply rooted in tradition, many nomadic tribes in the Sahara have had to adapt to the changing world. Over the past century, the rise of modern nation-states, colonialism, and the spread of modern technology have all had a profound impact on the nomadic lifestyle. Many governments have sought to settle nomadic populations, either through force or incentives, in an effort to exert greater control over their territories and provide modern services such as education, healthcare, and infrastructure. In some cases, nomadic tribes have been pushed to the margins of society, as their traditional way of life conflicts with modern state boundaries, land use, and economic development.

The discovery of oil, minerals, and other natural resources in the Sahara has also led to conflicts over land and resources, further complicating the lives of nomadic tribes. In some regions, the extraction of resources has led to environmental degradation, making it more difficult for nomads to find grazing land and water. In other areas, political instability, conflict, and the rise of armed groups have disrupted traditional trade routes and made travel more dangerous for nomads. Climate change, with its associated effects on rainfall patterns, desertification, and temperature extremes, poses another significant challenge to the nomadic lifestyle, as it threatens to further reduce the availability of water and grazing land in the Sahara.

Despite these challenges, many nomadic tribes in the Sahara have shown remarkable resilience and adaptability. Some have embraced modern technology, such as mobile phones, GPS, and solar power, to help them navigate the desert and communicate with the outside world. Others have diversified their livelihoods, incorporating farming, wage labor, and tourism into their traditional way of life. For example, some Tuareg and Bedouin tribes have become involved in the growing desert tourism industry, offering guided camel treks, cultural experiences, and desert camping to tourists seeking to experience the beauty and mystery of the Sahara.

In recent years, there has also been a renewed interest in preserving and promoting the cultural heritage of nomadic tribes in the Sahara. Festivals such as the Festival in the Desert, held in Mali, and the Ghat Festival, held in Libya, celebrate the music, dance, poetry, and traditions of the Tuareg and other desert peoples. These festivals provide an opportunity for nomadic tribes to share their culture with the world and connect with other communities, both within and outside the Sahara. Additionally, some nomadic groups have begun to organize politically, advocating for their rights to land, water, and cultural preservation in the face of modernization and globalization.

In conclusion, the nomadic tribes of the Sahara represent a unique and enduring way of life that has survived for thousands of years, despite the challenges posed by the desert's harsh environment and the pressures of the modern world. The Tuareg, Bedouin, Tubu, and other nomadic groups have developed sophisticated strategies for surviving in the Sahara, relying on their knowledge of the desert, their livestock, and their trading networks. While the future of the nomadic lifestyle is uncertain, these tribes have shown remarkable resilience and adaptability, and their cultural heritage continues to inspire and fascinate people around the world. As the Sahara continues to change, both environmentally and politically, the nomads of the desert will likely continue to play a vital role in shaping the region's future.

Chapter 9: The Great Sahara Desert Expeditions

The Great Sahara Desert expeditions represent some of the most remarkable and adventurous journeys in human history, showcasing mankind's enduring curiosity, resilience, and desire to explore the most extreme and inhospitable landscapes on Earth. The Sahara, stretching across North Africa, covers an area of about 9 million square kilometers, making it the largest hot desert in the world. Its vast and often harsh environment, with endless sand dunes, rocky plateaus, and arid plains, presents extreme challenges for any who dare to cross it. Over the centuries, explorers, traders, scientists, and adventurers have embarked on expeditions to traverse the Sahara, each with their own motives, ranging from the quest for knowledge to the search for fame, fortune, and scientific discovery. These expeditions have played a crucial role in uncovering the mysteries of the desert, mapping its features, and learning about its unique cultures and ecosystems. The stories of these expeditions are filled with tales of survival, endurance, and sometimes tragic loss, but they are also marked by moments of incredible discovery and human ingenuity.

One of the earliest recorded expeditions into the Sahara took place in the 5th century BCE, during the reign of the Carthaginian king Hanno the Navigator. Hanno's journey, though not as well documented as later expeditions, is one of the first known attempts by an ancient Mediterranean civilization to explore the Sahara and its surrounding regions. Carthage, located in present-day Tunisia, was a powerful city-state with extensive trade networks throughout the Mediterranean and Africa. Hanno's expedition was primarily a maritime voyage along the western coast of Africa, but it is believed that he also ventured inland into the desert, encountering indigenous peoples and exotic wildlife along the way. His journey, though shrouded in legend, helped establish trade routes that would later become important for the exchange of goods such as gold, ivory, and slaves between the Mediterranean world and sub-Saharan Africa.

Centuries later, during the Roman Empire, expeditions into the Sahara became more frequent as the empire sought to expand its influence into North Africa. The Romans were particularly interested in establishing control over the lucrative trade routes that passed through the desert, including the famous Trans-Saharan trade routes. These routes connected the Roman territories in North Africa with the wealthy and resource-rich kingdoms of sub-Saharan Africa, including the Kingdom of Ghana and later the Mali Empire. Roman expeditions into the Sahara were often military in nature, as the empire sought to protect its interests from nomadic tribes and other threats. However, these expeditions also provided valuable knowledge about the geography, climate, and peoples of the Sahara, laying the groundwork for future explorations.

By the Middle Ages, the Sahara had become a vital crossroads for trade and cultural exchange, with the Trans-Saharan trade routes facilitating the movement of goods such as gold, salt, spices, and textiles between North Africa and sub-Saharan Africa. The Muslim world, in particular, played a significant role in the exploration and documentation of the Sahara during this period. One of the most famous Muslim explorers to traverse the desert was the Moroccan traveler and scholar Ibn Battuta. Born in 1304, Ibn Battuta is often regarded as one of the greatest travelers in history, having journeyed across much of the known world, from North Africa to China, over the course of 30 years. His travels through the Sahara are particularly noteworthy, as they provide detailed accounts of the desert's geography, trade routes, and the various nomadic and settled peoples who inhabited the region. Ibn Battuta's descriptions of the Sahara offer a rare glimpse into life in the desert during the 14th century and highlight the importance of the Sahara as a cultural and economic bridge between Africa and the rest of the world.

The European exploration of the Sahara began in earnest during the Age of Exploration, particularly in the 18th and 19th centuries, when European powers became increasingly interested in mapping and controlling the vast African continent. European explorers, often sponsored by governments, scientific societies, or private patrons, ventured into the Sahara with a mix of curiosity, scientific ambition, and imperial ambition. These expeditions were fraught with danger, as the harsh desert environment, hostile nomadic tribes, and the vast, uncharted expanses of the Sahara presented significant challenges to even the most experienced adventurers.

One of the earliest and most famous European explorers of the Sahara was René Caillié, a French explorer who became the first European to return alive from the fabled city of Timbuktu, located on the edge of the Sahara in modern-day Mali. Born in 1799, Caillié grew up fascinated by tales of Timbuktu, which was rumored to be a city of immense wealth and cultural significance. At the time, little was known about Timbuktu by Europeans, as previous expeditions had either failed or ended in disaster. In 1827, Caillié set out from Senegal disguised as an Arab and spent several months traveling across the Sahara, enduring extreme heat, thirst, and danger from hostile tribes. After a grueling journey, he reached Timbuktu in 1828, only to find that the city was not the treasure trove of riches that many had imagined. Nevertheless, Caillié's successful return to Europe with detailed accounts of his journey earned him fame and recognition, and his expedition helped dispel many myths about the Sahara and its cities.

Another significant figure in the history of Saharan exploration is Heinrich Barth, a German explorer and scholar who undertook an extensive expedition through North Africa and the Sahara in the mid-19th century. Barth's journey, which lasted from 1850 to 1855, was one of the most comprehensive and scientifically significant explorations of the Sahara ever undertaken. Sponsored by the British government, Barth set out to explore the interior of Africa, mapping previously uncharted regions and documenting the cultures, languages, and histories of the peoples he encountered. His travels took him through present-day Libya, Niger, Chad, and Nigeria, and he became one of the first Europeans to explore the ancient city of Kano and the Lake Chad region. Barth's meticulous observations and detailed records of his journey were invaluable to the scientific community, and his work remains a key source of information about the Sahara and its peoples.

In addition to individual explorers, European colonial powers, particularly France and Britain, launched numerous expeditions into the Sahara during the 19th and early 20th centuries as part of their efforts to expand their empires in Africa. The French, in particular, were eager to establish control over the vast desert region and its trade routes, and they sent numerous military and scientific expeditions into the Sahara. One of the most notable French explorers was Charles de Foucauld, a former military officer who became a hermit and later a Christian missionary in the Sahara. De Foucauld's travels took him deep into the desert, where he lived among the Tuareg people and documented their language, culture, and way of life. His writings and maps contributed to the French understanding of the Sahara and its inhabitants, and his efforts to promote peace and understanding between Europeans and the Tuareg left a lasting legacy.

The 20th century saw continued interest in the exploration of the Sahara, particularly in the fields of geology, archaeology, and anthropology. As modern transportation and technology improved, scientists and researchers were able to conduct more detailed studies of the Sahara's geography, climate, and ecosystems. One of the most significant archaeological discoveries in the Sahara was the identification of prehistoric rock art in regions such as the Tassili n'Ajjer in Algeria and the Acacus Mountains in Libya. These ancient rock paintings and carvings, some of which date back more than 10,000 years, provide valuable insights into the Sahara's past, revealing that the region was once home to thriving human populations and a much wetter and more hospitable climate.

Modern expeditions into the Sahara have continued to uncover new information about the desert's history and natural environment. In recent decades, scientific expeditions have focused on studying the Sahara's changing climate, the movement of its sand dunes, and the preservation of its fragile ecosystems. Climate researchers have used satellite imagery and advanced technology to monitor desertification, the process by which fertile land becomes desert, and to track the Sahara's expansion over time. These studies are critical for understanding the broader impacts of climate change on both the Sahara and the surrounding regions, as desertification poses significant challenges for the people and wildlife who live in and around the Sahara.

In addition to scientific research, modern explorers and adventurers continue to be drawn to the Sahara's vast and mysterious landscapes. Expeditions today often involve crossing the desert by camel, 4x4 vehicles, or even on foot, with adventurers testing their endurance against the extreme conditions of the desert. These journeys, while often more recreational or symbolic than earlier expeditions, still require careful planning, preparation, and a deep respect for the desert's challenges. Some expeditions aim to raise awareness about environmental issues, such as desertification and water scarcity, while others seek to promote cultural understanding and preserve the traditional knowledge of the Sahara's nomadic peoples.

One of the most famous modern adventurers to cross the Sahara is Michael Asher, a British explorer and writer who has spent much of his life studying and living in the desert. Asher's numerous expeditions through the Sahara, often in the company of local nomads, have made him one of the leading authorities on the desert and its people. His journeys, documented in several books, highlight both the beauty and the dangers of the Sahara, as well as the resilience of the nomadic cultures that have survived there for centuries.

In conclusion, the great Sahara Desert expeditions represent a rich and diverse history of exploration, scientific discovery, and human endurance. From the ancient Carthaginians and Romans to medieval Muslim travelers and modern European explorers, each wave of exploration has contributed to our understanding of the Sahara and its place in the world. These expeditions have not only mapped the vast desert but also brought to light its unique cultures, ecosystems, and history. While the Sahara remains one of the most challenging environments on Earth, it continues to captivate the imagination of explorers, scientists, and adventurers alike. Today, the legacy of the great Sahara expeditions lives on, inspiring new generations to explore, study, and protect this magnificent and mysterious desert.

Chapter 10: The Oases of the Sahara Desert

The oases of the Sahara Desert are among the most remarkable and essential features of this vast, arid region. Scattered like islands of life in a sea of sand, these oases are critical lifelines, supporting human settlements, agriculture, and wildlife in an otherwise harsh and inhospitable environment. For millennia, oases have been key to survival in the Sahara, providing the water, shade, and fertile land necessary for sustaining life in one of the driest places on Earth. They have played a pivotal role in shaping the cultures, economies, and histories of the people who live in and around the desert, serving as hubs of trade, centers of agriculture, and places of refuge for travelers and nomads.

The formation of oases in the Sahara is a result of specific geological and environmental factors. Beneath the vast desert, there are underground aquifers—ancient reserves of water that have accumulated over thousands, if not millions, of years. These aquifers are remnants from a time when the Sahara was much wetter and supported rivers, lakes, and lush vegetation. As the desert's climate changed and became more arid, surface water sources dried up, but underground aquifers remained, trapped beneath layers of rock and sand. In some places, these aquifers come close to the surface or are exposed due to geological formations, allowing water to rise and form springs. These springs, in turn, feed into natural depressions in the landscape, creating small areas of fertile land where plant life can grow and flourish. In other cases, humans have tapped into these underground water sources through the construction of wells, making it possible to establish permanent settlements in the desert.

Oases are typically found in low-lying areas such as basins, depressions, and the bases of mountains, where rainwater runoff can accumulate or where underground water is more accessible. The size of an oasis can vary widely, from a small patch of greenery surrounding a single spring or well, to larger, more extensive areas of cultivation and habitation that support entire communities. The water in an oasis allows for the growth of crops, which is crucial for both the local population and the travelers who rely on these green havens during long desert journeys. The ability to cultivate crops such as dates, olives, wheat, barley, and various fruits and vegetables has been central to the sustainability of human life in the Sahara. Date palms, in particular, are a common sight in Saharan oases and have been cultivated for thousands of years. These hardy trees thrive in the hot desert climate and can grow in sandy, nutrient-poor soils. Their deep roots can reach the underground water supply, while their tall, sturdy trunks and broad leaves provide shade for other plants and animals. Dates are not only a staple food for the local populations but also an important trade commodity, as they can be dried and preserved for long periods, making them ideal for long desert journeys.

One of the most famous oases in the Sahara is the Siwa Oasis, located in western Egypt, near the Libyan border. Siwa is one of the most isolated and historically significant oases in the Sahara, with a unique culture and history that dates back to ancient times. The Siwa Oasis is fed by several springs and wells, and its fertile land supports a thriving agricultural community, with date palms, olive trees, and various fruits and vegetables being cultivated in abundance. Siwa is also known for its ancient ruins, including the Temple of the Oracle of Amun, which was famously visited by Alexander the Great in 331 BCE. The Siwa Oasis has long been a crossroads for trade and cultural exchange, and it has played a significant role in the history of the region, serving as a vital stopover for caravans traveling between North Africa and the Nile Valley.

Another prominent oasis in the Sahara is the Ghadames Oasis, located in western Libya, near the borders of Tunisia and Algeria.

Ghadames is one of the oldest continuously inhabited places in the Sahara, with a history that dates back more than 2,000 years. The oasis is situated in a natural depression surrounded by mountains, which helps to trap and retain water from underground sources. The city of Ghadames, built around the oasis, is a UNESCO World Heritage site and is renowned for its unique architecture, with whitewashed houses made of mud, lime, and palm wood. The city's narrow, winding streets and covered walkways provide shade and protection from the intense desert heat, creating a cool, sheltered environment for its inhabitants. The Ghadames Oasis has long been a center of trade and commerce, with caravans passing through on their way to and from the Mediterranean coast, sub-Saharan Africa, and the interior of the Sahara.

In Algeria, the M'zab Valley is home to a series of oases that have supported human settlements for over a thousand years. The valley is located in the northern part of the Sahara and is fed by underground water sources that allow for the cultivation of date palms and other crops. The M'zab Valley is famous for its unique architectural and cultural heritage, with the five fortified towns (known as ksour) of the Ibadi Muslim community forming a distinctive landscape. The towns, including Ghardaïa, are built around oases, and their architecture is designed to protect the inhabitants from both the desert heat and potential invaders. The M'zab Valley is a UNESCO World Heritage site, recognized for its cultural and historical significance.

Farther south, in the central Sahara, the Kufra Oasis in southeastern Libya is another notable example of a desert oasis. Kufra is a large oasis complex that consists of several smaller oases, fed by both natural springs and wells. Kufra has long been a key stop on the trans-Saharan trade routes, particularly for caravans carrying slaves, gold, ivory, and other goods between sub-Saharan Africa and the Mediterranean world. The oasis is also home to the indigenous Tubu people, who have traditionally relied on the oasis for agriculture and as a base for their nomadic lifestyle. Kufra's strategic location and its abundant water supply have made it a crucial outpost in the vast, otherwise barren stretches of the Sahara.

In addition to the major oases, there are countless smaller oases scattered throughout the Sahara, each playing a vital role in supporting local populations, wildlife, and nomadic tribes. Many of these oases have long been inhabited by Berber, Tuareg, and other nomadic peoples who have developed deep knowledge of the desert and its resources. These nomadic groups have traditionally relied on oases not only for water and food but also as places of refuge during their long migrations across the desert. The Tuareg, for example, have historically controlled many of the oases in the central Sahara, using them as bases for their camel caravans, which transported goods across the desert.

Oases have also played a crucial role in the history of trans-Saharan trade. For centuries, caravans of camels would traverse the vast distances between North Africa and sub-Saharan Africa, carrying goods such as gold, salt, ivory, spices, and textiles. The oases served as essential stopping points on these long journeys, providing water and shelter for both the traders and their animals. The trade routes that passed through the Sahara were vital for connecting the economies of West Africa with the Mediterranean world and the Middle East. The wealth generated by this trade helped to build powerful empires such as the Mali Empire, which controlled key oases and trade routes in the western Sahara.

The importance of oases in the Sahara cannot be overstated, as they are not only centers of life but also cultural and economic hubs. Many oases have been the sites of ancient cities and settlements, some of which date back thousands of years. These cities often developed into thriving centers of trade, religion, and learning, attracting scholars, merchants, and travelers from across the region. The cities of Timbuktu and Gao, for example, were both located near the edge of the Sahara and were important centers of Islamic scholarship and trade during the medieval period. While not technically within the desert, these cities relied on the nearby oases to support their populations and sustain trade networks that stretched across the Sahara.

The ecology of oases is also unique, as they support a wide range of plant and animal life that is otherwise scarce in the desert. In addition to date palms, which are the most common crop grown in oases, a variety of other plants thrive in these fertile pockets. Fruits such as figs, pomegranates, and apricots are often grown, along with vegetables like onions, tomatoes, and beans. The availability of water and shade in oases creates a microclimate that supports more diverse ecosystems than the surrounding desert. Birds, insects, and small mammals are often found in and around oases, taking advantage of the food and water sources provided by the lush vegetation. In some cases, oases also serve as important stopover points for migratory birds traveling across the Sahara.

Despite their importance, the oases of the Sahara face significant challenges, particularly in the modern era. Climate change, desertification, and over-extraction of water from underground aquifers are all serious threats to the sustainability of oases. As the Sahara continues to expand due to desertification, many oases are at risk of drying up or becoming less productive. The overuse of water for agriculture, particularly in larger oases, has led to a depletion of groundwater reserves, making it harder to sustain crops and livestock. In some cases, traditional irrigation systems, such as *foggaras* (underground channels that transport water from the aquifer to the fields), have fallen into disrepair or been replaced by less sustainable methods of water extraction.

In response to these challenges, there have been efforts to protect and conserve the oases of the Sahara. Local communities, governments, and international organizations have worked to promote sustainable water management practices, restore traditional irrigation systems, and reduce the impact of desertification. In some areas, reforestation projects have been undertaken to help stabilize the soil and prevent further encroachment of the desert. Additionally, there has been a growing recognition of the cultural and historical significance of oases, with many oases being designated as UNESCO World Heritage sites or protected areas.

In conclusion, the oases of the Sahara Desert are truly remarkable and indispensable features of this vast, arid region. They provide the water, shade, and fertile land necessary to support human life, agriculture, and wildlife in one of the harshest environments on Earth. Oases have been central to the development of trade, culture, and civilization in the Sahara for thousands of years, serving as hubs of commerce, agriculture, and learning. While they face significant challenges in the modern era, oases remain vital to the survival of the people and ecosystems of the Sahara, and efforts to protect and sustain these lifelines will be crucial for the future of the desert.

Chapter 11: The Sahara's Mysterious Rock Art

The Sahara's mysterious rock art is one of the most fascinating and evocative remnants of the desert's ancient past, offering a glimpse into a time when the now barren landscape was teeming with life and human activity. These rock paintings and carvings, which date back thousands of years, are scattered across the desert in regions such as Algeria's Tassili n'Ajjer, Libya's Tadrart Acacus, and Niger's Aïr Mountains. Created by early inhabitants of the Sahara, the artwork portrays a vibrant and thriving environment that was once far greener and wetter than the arid desert we know today. These ancient images of people, animals, and enigmatic symbols provide a unique window into the lives, beliefs, and cultures of the desert's prehistoric inhabitants. Yet, despite the wealth of information they offer, many questions about the creators of the rock art, their motivations, and the exact meaning of the images remain shrouded in mystery.

The discovery of Saharan rock art in the modern era began in the mid-19th century, when European explorers traveling through the desert encountered strange and beautiful drawings and carvings etched into the cliffs and boulders of the Sahara's remote landscapes. However, it wasn't until the early 20th century that systematic study of the rock art began, largely thanks to the efforts of French archaeologist Henri Lhote, who conducted extensive research in the Tassili n'Ajjer region of southeastern Algeria. Lhote and his team uncovered thousands of rock paintings, which depicted a wide array of human figures, animals, and abstract symbols. His work sparked global interest in the ancient art of the Sahara, leading to further research and the realization that this art was part of a larger prehistoric tradition that stretched across much of North Africa.

One of the most striking aspects of the Sahara's rock art is the range of animals depicted in the images, many of which no longer exist in the region today. Giraffes, elephants, rhinoceroses, hippos, and antelopes feature prominently in the artwork, suggesting that the Sahara was once home to a much more diverse ecosystem than the barren desert landscape of the present. These animals are often shown in detailed and naturalistic poses, as if frozen in time: giraffes stretching their long necks toward the leaves of trees, elephants grazing in the savannah, or herds of antelopes racing across open plains. The presence of these animals in the rock art is a powerful reminder that the Sahara was once a much greener and wetter place, a region covered by lakes, rivers, and savannahs where both humans and wildlife thrived. This is supported by geological and climate research, which indicates that during the African Humid Period, which lasted roughly from 10,000 to 5,000 years ago, the Sahara experienced much higher levels of rainfall, supporting vast grasslands, forests, and even large lakes.

In addition to the animals, the rock art also frequently depicts human figures engaged in a variety of activities, including hunting, dancing, herding, and ritual practices. In some scenes, human figures are shown wearing elaborate headdresses or holding weapons such as bows and arrows, suggesting a highly developed culture with complex social and religious practices. The images of people hunting animals, often with the help of dogs, are particularly common, highlighting the importance of hunting to the early inhabitants of the Sahara. In other scenes, figures are shown tending to herds of cattle, goats, or sheep, which indicates that pastoralism became a significant way of life for these ancient people as the environment gradually became more arid. The rock art thus provides evidence of the shift from a primarily hunter-gatherer lifestyle to one based on animal husbandry and agriculture as the Sahara's climate changed over time.

One of the most enigmatic and debated aspects of the Sahara's rock art is the depiction of mysterious, otherworldly figures that have come to be known as "round-headed" or "alien-like" figures. These figures, which are particularly common in the Tassili n'Ajjer region, are characterized by large, round heads, often with no discernible facial features, and elongated bodies. Some of these figures appear to be wearing strange clothing or headgear, and they are sometimes shown in association with symbols or animals that seem to have ritual or symbolic significance. These unusual figures have sparked considerable speculation among scholars and enthusiasts alike, with some suggesting that they represent shamanistic practices or religious rituals, while others have posited more far-fetched theories, including the idea that they could represent extraterrestrial beings. Despite these theories, the true meaning of the round-headed figures remains a mystery, and they continue to intrigue researchers and the public alike.

The Sahara's rock art can be divided into several distinct styles or phases, each of which corresponds to different periods of the region's prehistory. The oldest of these phases, known as the "Round Head Period," is believed to date back as far as 10,000 to 12,000 years ago and is characterized by the round-headed figures mentioned earlier. These early artworks are often found in the most remote and inaccessible parts of the desert, suggesting that they may have been created by the earliest human inhabitants of the region, possibly as part of religious or shamanistic rituals. The Round Head Period is followed by the "Bovidian Period," which dates from around 7,000 to 4,000 years ago and is named for the prominent depictions of cattle (bovines) in the rock art of this time. This period marks the transition from a hunter-gatherer society to a more pastoral way of life, with an emphasis on the domestication of animals, particularly cattle, which were of great economic and social importance to the people of the time. The artwork from this period shows scenes of cattle herding, milking, and even what appear to be ritual activities centered around the animals, suggesting that cattle held a special place in the culture and religion of these early Saharan peoples.

The final major phase of Saharan rock art is known as the "Horse and Chariot Period," which dates from around 3,000 to 2,000 years ago and reflects the introduction of horses and wheeled vehicles into the region. This period corresponds to the beginning of the desertification of the Sahara, as the climate became increasingly arid and the once fertile land turned into the desert we see today. The arrival of horses, and later chariots, into the Sahara from the Mediterranean and Near East marked a significant cultural shift, as these animals revolutionized transportation and warfare in the region. The rock art from this period often shows figures riding horses or driving chariots, sometimes in scenes of conflict or warfare. This reflects the growing importance of horses in the societies of the time and suggests that the Sahara was becoming a more contested and volatile region as resources became scarcer and people were forced to compete for land and water.

One of the most significant and well-preserved collections of rock art in the Sahara is located in the Tassili n'Ajjer region of southeastern Algeria, a UNESCO World Heritage site. The Tassili n'Ajjer is a vast plateau of sandstone that is home to thousands of rock paintings and carvings, some of which are over 10,000 years old. The artwork here is incredibly diverse, with depictions of animals, humans, and abstract symbols covering the walls of caves and cliffs throughout the region. The isolation and inaccessibility of the Tassili n'Ajjer have helped to preserve the rock art, making it one of the most important archaeological sites in Africa. The region's dramatic landscapes of eroded sandstone formations, deep gorges, and natural rock shelters have created the perfect canvas for these ancient artists, and the sheer number of artworks in the area has led some to refer to it as an "open-air museum."

The Tadrart Acacus in southwestern Libya is another important site for Saharan rock art. Like the Tassili n'Ajjer, the Acacus is a region of rugged sandstone mountains that have been sculpted by wind and water over millennia, creating an otherworldly landscape of cliffs, caves, and natural arches. The rock art in the Tadrart Acacus dates back to around 12,000 years ago and includes depictions of animals, humans, and abstract symbols, with a particular emphasis on the wildlife that once roamed the area, such as giraffes, elephants, and antelopes. The artwork here is noted for its vivid colors and detailed representations, providing a rich visual record of life in the Sahara during the African Humid Period.

In Niger, the Aïr Mountains are home to another significant collection of rock art, much of which dates from the Bovidian and Horse and Chariot periods. The Aïr Mountains are a rugged range of volcanic peaks and plateaus that rise dramatically from the surrounding desert, and the rock art here reflects the changing environment and lifestyles of the people who lived in the region. As in other parts of the Sahara, the rock art of the Aïr Mountains includes depictions of cattle, horses, and chariots, as well as scenes of hunting and pastoral life. The artwork here provides important insights into the cultural and economic changes that took place in the Sahara as the climate became drier and people adapted to the increasingly harsh conditions.

Despite the wealth of information that Saharan rock art offers, much remains unknown about the people who created it. Archaeological evidence suggests that the Sahara was home to a number of different cultures and ethnic groups over the millennia, each of which contributed to the region's artistic traditions. However, because these prehistoric peoples left no written records, much of what we know about them comes from their art and the few artifacts that have been uncovered in the region. The purpose of the rock art is also the subject of ongoing debate among scholars. Some researchers believe that the artwork served primarily as a form of communication or storytelling, perhaps recording important events, rituals, or myths. Others suggest that the art may have had a religious or spiritual function, with certain sites serving as sacred spaces where people gathered to perform rituals or ceremonies.

In recent years, advances in technology have allowed researchers to study Saharan rock art in greater detail than ever before. Techniques such as radiocarbon dating, digital imaging, and satellite mapping have provided new insights into the age, distribution, and meaning of the artwork. For example, radiocarbon dating of organic materials found at rock art sites has helped to establish more accurate timelines for the creation of the art, while digital imaging has revealed previously hidden details and patterns in the artwork. Satellite mapping has also allowed researchers to identify new rock art sites in remote and inaccessible areas of the desert, opening up new opportunities for exploration and study.

In conclusion, the Sahara's mysterious rock art is a rich and captivating testament to the desert's ancient past. It provides a visual record of the changing environment, cultures, and lifestyles of the people who once lived in this vast region, offering valuable insights into their world. From the depictions of now-extinct animals to the enigmatic round-headed figures and the scenes of pastoral life, the rock art of the Sahara is a window into a time when the desert was a much different place, teeming with life and activity. Despite the many mysteries that still surround this ancient artwork, ongoing research continues to shed light on the people who created it and the world they inhabited, ensuring that the legacy of the Sahara's prehistoric artists endures for generations to come.

Chapter 12: The Sahara's Role in Trade and Travel

The Sahara Desert, though often imagined as an inhospitable, barren landscape, has played an enormous role in trade and travel throughout history. Far from being a barrier between civilizations, the Sahara has served as a vast bridge connecting different parts of Africa with each other and with regions as far away as Europe and the Middle East. The desert's immense size, covering around 9.2 million square kilometers, and its harsh climate did not deter early traders and travelers; instead, it became a bustling highway for commerce, culture, and knowledge. In the ancient and medieval periods, the Sahara's trade routes were among the most important in the world, fostering economic, cultural, and political exchanges that had a lasting impact on the development of civilizations across North Africa, West Africa, and beyond. The Sahara has been both a challenge and a lifeline, a place where intrepid traders, explorers, and nomads could cross vast distances, connecting the peoples and resources of distant lands.

The importance of the Sahara as a trade route dates back thousands of years, with evidence of early trade and travel activities going as far back as 4,000 to 5,000 years. However, it was during the first millennium CE that the Sahara truly came into its own as a major conduit for trade, particularly with the rise of trans-Saharan trade routes. These routes crisscrossed the desert, linking the northern Mediterranean coast with sub-Saharan Africa. Caravans of camels, known as "ships of the desert," carried goods such as gold, salt, ivory, textiles, and slaves across the treacherous expanse of the desert, facilitating the movement of wealth and resources between regions.

One of the key factors that enabled trade across the Sahara was the domestication of the camel around the 3rd century CE. Camels, with their remarkable ability to endure the extreme heat and arid conditions of the desert, revolutionized travel and trade. Their ability to store water and fat allowed them to trek for days without needing sustenance, making them ideal for long journeys across the inhospitable landscape. Before the use of camels, attempts to cross the Sahara had been limited, as the distances were too vast, and the desert's conditions too harsh, for horses and other animals to survive the trip. The introduction of camels, therefore, opened up new possibilities for trade and allowed for the establishment of regular trans-Saharan trade routes.

The most famous of these trade routes was the Trans-Saharan Caravan Route, which connected the great empires of West Africa, such as the Ghana Empire, Mali Empire, and Songhai Empire, with the Mediterranean and the Arab world. Gold, mined in the forests and rivers of West Africa, was one of the most valuable commodities transported along these routes. West African gold was in high demand in the Mediterranean and Middle Eastern markets, where it was used to mint coins, craft luxury items, and support the wealth of powerful states and empires. In return, traders from the north brought salt, a highly prized commodity in West Africa, where it was essential for preserving food and maintaining health. The salt mines of the Sahara, particularly those at Taghaza, were major sources of wealth, and caravans of camels would carry large blocks of salt across the desert to be traded in the markets of West Africa.

Alongside gold and salt, the Sahara's trade routes facilitated the exchange of other goods such as ivory, slaves, horses, and textiles. West Africa's ivory, harvested from the tusks of elephants, was sought after for its use in art, jewelry, and ceremonial objects in both Europe and the Middle East. Slaves, unfortunately, were another significant commodity in trans-Saharan trade, with many being captured in wars or raids and sold to traders who would transport them across the desert to be sold in the markets of North Africa or the Mediterranean. The textiles that flowed into West Africa from the Mediterranean and

Middle East included fine silks, cottons, and woolen fabrics, which were highly prized for their quality and craftsmanship. Horses were another important item of trade, as they were valued in West Africa for their role in warfare and transportation.

The wealth generated by trans-Saharan trade had a profound impact on the rise of powerful states and empires in both West Africa and North Africa. The Ghana Empire, which flourished from the 6th to the 13th century, was one of the earliest West African empires to benefit from the gold-salt trade. The empire controlled several key trade routes across the Sahara and taxed the caravans that passed through its territory, amassing great wealth in the process. The later Mali Empire, which reached its peak in the 13th and 14th centuries, became even more prosperous thanks to its control of gold mines and its strategic location along the trade routes. Mansa Musa, the ruler of Mali, became legendary for his wealth, which was largely derived from the trans-Saharan trade. During his famous pilgrimage to Mecca in 1324, Mansa Musa distributed so much gold along the way that he caused inflation in the regions he visited. The Songhai Empire, which succeeded Mali in the 15th and 16th centuries, also owed much of its power and wealth to the control of trade routes and the goods that flowed through the Sahara.

The Sahara's role in trade was not just about the exchange of goods, but also about the transmission of culture, knowledge, and religion. The caravans that traversed the desert were not only laden with commodities but also with ideas, art, and beliefs. Islamic scholars, traders, and missionaries traveled along the same routes as the caravans, spreading the teachings of Islam to the peoples of West Africa. By the 11th century, Islam had taken root in many of the urban centers of West Africa, such as Timbuktu, Gao, and Djenne, which became important centers of Islamic learning and scholarship. Timbuktu, in particular, became renowned for its universities and libraries, which attracted scholars from across the Islamic world. The trans-Saharan trade routes thus played a key role in the Islamization of West Africa and the spread of Islamic culture and learning throughout the region.

In addition to Islam, the Sahara's trade routes facilitated the exchange of artistic traditions, architectural styles, and technological innovations. Artifacts such as pottery, jewelry, and metalwork show clear influences from both North Africa and sub-Saharan Africa, demonstrating the cultural interconnections fostered by trade. Architectural styles, particularly in cities like Timbuktu and Gao, reflect a blending of Saharan, North African, and West African influences, with features such as mud-brick buildings, flat roofs, and intricately carved wooden doors becoming characteristic of the region. Technological innovations, such as improved methods of irrigation and agriculture, also spread along the trade routes, helping to sustain the populations of the desert and the regions beyond.

Despite its importance, travel across the Sahara was never easy. The desert's extreme heat, vast distances, and lack of water made it a perilous journey. Caravans would often travel at night to avoid the searing daytime temperatures, navigating by the stars to find their way across the featureless expanses of sand and rock. The journey could take weeks or even months, depending on the route and the size of the caravan, and travelers faced the constant threat of sandstorms, dehydration, and attacks by bandits. Oases, scattered throughout the desert, were essential lifelines, providing water, food, and shelter for both travelers and their animals. These oases, such as those at Ghadames, Siwa, and Bilma, became important hubs of trade and communication, where merchants could rest, replenish their supplies, and exchange goods before continuing their journey.

The arrival of European explorers in the Sahara in the 19th century marked a new chapter in the desert's history of travel and trade. Motivated by a desire to map the region, find new trade routes, and expand colonial empires, European explorers such as René Caillié, Heinrich Barth, and Mungo Park undertook perilous journeys across the desert, often with the assistance of local guides and caravans. These expeditions opened up new knowledge of the Sahara's geography, peoples, and resources, although they also paved the way for European colonization and exploitation of the region.

In the modern era, the Sahara's role in trade and travel has evolved. While traditional camel caravans are no longer the primary means of transportation, the Sahara remains an important route for the movement of goods, people, and ideas. Modern highways and air routes now crisscross the desert, facilitating trade between North Africa, sub-Saharan Africa, and the wider world. The extraction of natural resources, such as oil, gas, and minerals, has become a major industry in the Sahara, attracting investment and infrastructure development in countries such as Algeria, Libya, and Niger. Meanwhile, the Sahara has also become a destination for adventure tourism, with travelers from around the world drawn to the desert's stunning landscapes, ancient history, and vibrant cultures.

In conclusion, the Sahara Desert has played a pivotal role in trade and travel throughout history, serving as a vast and challenging highway that connected distant regions and civilizations. From the early days of trans-Saharan trade, when camel caravans transported gold, salt, and other commodities across the desert, to the spread of Islam and the exchange of culture, knowledge, and ideas, the Sahara has been a vital conduit for human interaction. Despite its harsh conditions, the desert has fostered the growth of powerful empires, facilitated the exchange of goods and cultures, and connected the peoples of Africa, Europe, and the Middle East. Today, the Sahara continues to be a region of economic and cultural significance, a testament to the enduring role of this vast desert in shaping the course of history.

Chapter 13: Unique Plants of the Sahara Desert

The Sahara Desert, often perceived as a barren and inhospitable landscape due to its extreme heat and aridity, is in fact home to an array of unique plant species that have adapted to survive the harsh conditions of this vast and unforgiving environment. While the Sahara is the largest hot desert in the world, spanning approximately 9.2 million square kilometers across North Africa, from the Atlantic Ocean in the west to the Red Sea in the east, and from the Mediterranean Sea in the north to the Sahel in the south, its ecosystem is far from lifeless. The extreme climate, characterized by scorching daytime temperatures, freezing nights, and a near-complete absence of rainfall, presents immense challenges for plant life. Yet, a variety of plants have evolved remarkable adaptations that allow them not only to survive but to thrive in this desert environment. These plants are often resilient, resourceful, and highly specialized, with unique features that have fascinated botanists and desert explorers for centuries.

One of the most well-known groups of plants in the Sahara is the xerophytes, a term that refers to plants that are specially adapted to live in extremely dry conditions. These plants have developed various strategies to conserve water, such as reducing their leaf surface area, storing water in their tissues, or developing extensive root systems that can tap into underground moisture reserves. Some of the most iconic xerophytes of the Sahara include species like the date palm, acacia, and various types of cacti and succulents. The ability to withstand prolonged periods without water is a hallmark of desert plants, and these species exemplify how life can persist even in the most arid of environments.

The date palm (Phoenix dactylifera) is perhaps one of the most famous and important plants of the Sahara, not only for its ecological role but also for its cultural and economic significance. Date palms are often found around oases, where underground water sources provide the necessary moisture for these trees to grow. The date palm is a hardy species, able to tolerate both extreme heat and long periods of drought. Its deep roots allow it to access water from the water table far below the desert surface, while its long, arching fronds provide shade and help reduce water loss by minimizing evaporation from the ground. In addition to providing shade and shelter, the date palm is a valuable source of food for desert communities. Its fruits, dates, are rich in sugars, vitamins, and minerals, making them an important staple food in many parts of the Sahara. The tree's leaves and fibers are also used to make a variety of products, including baskets, mats, and ropes, highlighting the date palm's versatility and importance in sustaining life in the desert.

Another significant group of plants in the Sahara is the acacia species, such as the Acacia tortilis (umbrella thorn) and Acacia raddiana. These trees are adapted to survive in the dry, nutrient-poor soils of the desert and play a crucial role in the desert ecosystem. Acacias are known for their tough, thorny branches and small, feathery leaves, which reduce water loss through transpiration. These trees have deep root systems that allow them to access underground water reserves, and some species are capable of shedding their leaves during the driest months to conserve moisture. Acacias provide food and shelter for a variety of desert animals, including camels, goats, and birds, and their seeds are an important food source for many species. Additionally, acacias help to stabilize desert soils and prevent erosion, making them key players in maintaining the fragile desert environment.

Succulent plants, including various species of cacti and other desert-adapted succulents, are another important group of plants in the Sahara. Succulents are known for their ability to store water in their thick, fleshy leaves, stems, or roots, which allows them to survive long periods of drought. One such succulent that is native to the Sahara is the Saharan aloe (Aloe saharae). This plant has thick, spiny leaves that store water and help the plant endure the extreme heat and dryness of the desert. The Saharan aloe, like other members of the aloe family, produces a gel that is used for its medicinal properties, particularly in treating burns and skin conditions. Its ability to store water makes it a model of desert survival, allowing it to flourish in an environment where water is incredibly scarce.

In addition to these well-known plants, the Sahara is home to a variety of less conspicuous but equally fascinating species that have evolved to cope with the harsh desert conditions. One example is the thyme-leaved sandwort (Arenaria serpyllifolia), a small, herbaceous plant that grows in sandy or rocky soils. This plant has tiny, narrow leaves that reduce water loss, and its small size allows it to remain close to the ground, where it is less exposed to the harsh winds and intense sunlight of the desert. Despite its unassuming appearance, the thyme-leaved sandwort is an important part of the desert ecosystem, providing food for herbivores and contributing to soil stabilization.

The Sahara is also home to several species of grasses that have adapted to the desert's challenging conditions. One such grass is the desert grass (Stipagrostis pungens), which grows in sandy soils and plays a crucial role in stabilizing sand dunes. The plant's long, slender leaves reduce water loss, and its deep root system helps anchor the plant in place, preventing the shifting sands from engulfing it. Desert grasses like Stipagrostis are important not only for their role in stabilizing the desert environment but also for providing food and habitat for desert animals, particularly herbivores such as gazelles and camels.

Among the more unusual plants of the Sahara is the Argan tree (Argania spinosa), native to the region between the Sahara and the Mediterranean. This hardy tree is well-adapted to drought and poor soils, and it is known for its ability to survive in extreme conditions. The Argan tree is famous for producing argan oil, a valuable product used in cosmetics, cooking, and traditional medicine. The tree's fruits contain a hard kernel from which the oil is extracted, and it is considered a vital economic resource for local communities, particularly in Morocco. Argan trees are also important for preventing desertification, as they help to maintain soil structure and prevent erosion.

Ephemeral plants are another fascinating group that thrive in the Sahara's unpredictable environment. These plants have adapted to take full advantage of the brief periods of rainfall that occur in the desert, growing, flowering, and producing seeds in a matter of days or weeks after the rains. Once the rains arrive, the seeds of these plants, which may have lain dormant in the soil for months or even years, germinate rapidly, allowing the plants to complete their life cycle before the moisture evaporates. These ephemeral plants include species like the desert marigold (Calendula arvensis) and the desert hyacinth (Cistanche tubulosa), which bloom quickly and bring a burst of color to the otherwise barren landscape. Their seeds are specially adapted to survive long periods of drought, ensuring the continuation of the species even in the most extreme conditions.

Halophytes, or salt-tolerant plants, are another unique group of plants found in the Sahara, particularly around salt flats and saline environments. These plants have adapted to survive in soils with high salt concentrations, which would be toxic to most other plants. One example of a halophyte in the Sahara is the saltbush (Atriplex halimus), a shrub that can grow in highly saline soils and is capable of excreting excess salt through specialized glands in its leaves. Saltbush is an important food source for livestock, particularly in regions where other vegetation is scarce, and it also plays a role in soil stabilization and preventing erosion in saline areas.

A particularly interesting example of desert adaptation is found in the Welwitschia mirabilis, a plant native to the Namib Desert, which borders the southern edge of the Sahara. While not exclusive to the Sahara itself, the Welwitschia is often cited as one of the most unique and long-living plants of any desert environment. This strange plant consists of only two leaves that continue to grow throughout its entire lifespan, which can span over 1,000 years. The leaves spread out over the ground, absorbing moisture from dew and fog, which are critical sources of water in the arid desert environment. The Welwitschia's incredible resilience and longevity make it a symbol of the Sahara's and surrounding deserts' plant survival strategies.

In addition to these more familiar plants, the Sahara is home to several rare and endemic species that are found nowhere else in the world. One such species is the Saharan cypress (Cupressus dupreziana), a critically endangered tree that grows in the Tassili n'Ajjer region of Algeria. This species is highly adapted to the desert's harsh conditions, able to survive on very little water and in nutrient-poor soils. However, due to habitat loss and climate change, the Saharan cypress is now one of the rarest trees on Earth, with only a few hundred individuals remaining in the wild.

Another unique plant found in the Sahara is the desert rose (Adenium obesum), a succulent shrub known for its striking appearance and bright pink or red flowers. Despite its beauty, the desert rose is well-adapted to the extreme heat and drought of the desert, storing water in its swollen, bulbous stem to help it survive during dry periods. The desert rose is highly valued as an ornamental plant, both in the Sahara and around the world, and it is often cultivated for its attractive flowers and distinctive form.

Despite the Sahara's reputation as a lifeless expanse of sand, it is home to a surprisingly diverse array of plant species, each of which has evolved unique adaptations to survive the desert's harsh conditions. From the towering date palms and resilient acacias to the water-storing succulents and fast-blooming ephemerals, the plants of the Sahara are a testament to the resilience of life in one of the most extreme environments on Earth. These plants play a vital role in supporting the desert's ecosystem, providing food, shelter, and stability in a landscape where survival is a constant challenge. Moreover, they offer valuable resources to the human populations that have lived in and around the Sahara for millennia, contributing to both the ecological and cultural richness of the region.

Chapter 14: The Hidden Mountains of the Sahara

The Sahara Desert, known primarily for its vast expanses of shifting sand dunes and its extreme climate, hides within its boundaries several mountain ranges that are both awe-inspiring and mysterious. These hidden mountains of the Sahara are often overlooked in popular depictions of the desert, which tend to focus on its endless, barren landscapes of sand and rock. However, these rugged, towering peaks offer a glimpse into a very different aspect of the Sahara's geography, one that is rich in geological history, biodiversity, and human culture. Far from being uniform or monotonous, the Sahara's landscape is punctuated by mountain ranges that rise dramatically from the desert floor, some of which are home to unique ecosystems and have played an important role in the history of the people who have lived in or passed through the region. These mountains, often isolated and remote, add a layer of intrigue to the Sahara, making it not just the world's largest hot desert, but also a place of hidden natural wonders.

The most famous and significant of these mountain ranges is the Ahaggar Mountains, also known as the Hoggar Mountains, located in the southern part of Algeria. The Ahaggar range is one of the largest and most imposing mountain systems in the Sahara, with peaks that reach over 3,000 meters (9,800 feet) above sea level. The range covers an area of approximately 550,000 square kilometers and consists of rugged volcanic rock formations, deep valleys, and steep cliffs that create a dramatic and surreal landscape. The Ahaggar Mountains are primarily composed of ancient volcanic rocks that date back to the Precambrian period, making them some of the oldest geological formations in the Sahara. The highest peak in the Ahaggar range is Mount Tahat, which stands at 2,918 meters (9,573 feet) and is the highest point in Algeria.

One of the most fascinating aspects of the Ahaggar Mountains is their role as a haven for life in an otherwise harsh and unforgiving desert environment. The higher elevations of the Ahaggar range experience cooler temperatures and receive more rainfall than the surrounding desert, creating microclimates that support a surprising diversity of plant and animal species. The valleys and plateaus of the Ahaggar are home to species such as the Barbary sheep, fennec fox, and various birds of prey, which find refuge in the rocky outcrops and canyons. The presence of permanent springs and water sources in the Ahaggar Mountains has also allowed human populations to inhabit the region for thousands of years. The Tuareg people, a semi-nomadic Berber group, have lived in the Ahaggar Mountains for centuries, and the range remains an important cultural and spiritual center for them. The city of Tamanrasset, located at the foot of the mountains, serves as a gateway to the range and is a key stop for travelers and traders crossing the central Sahara.

The Ahaggar Mountains are not just a natural wonder; they are also steeped in human history and mythology. The mountains are considered sacred by the Tuareg people, who view them as the dwelling place of their ancestors and the seat of their cultural identity. According to Tuareg legend, the mountains were the home of Tin Hinan, a mythical queen who is said to be the ancestor of all Tuareg people. Tin Hinan's tomb, which was discovered in the Ahaggar Mountains in the 1920s, has become an important archaeological site and is regarded as a symbol of Tuareg heritage. The tomb, which contains the remains of a woman who was buried with jewelry and other artifacts, is believed to date back to the 4th or 5th century CE, further cementing the historical significance of the Ahaggar range.

Moving westward, another hidden mountain range in the Sahara is the Tibesti Mountains, located in northern Chad and extending into southern Libya. The Tibesti range is one of the most remote and least explored regions of the Sahara, and it is home to some of the highest peaks in the desert. The highest point in the Tibesti Mountains, and in all of the Sahara, is Emi Koussi, a massive shield volcano that rises to an elevation of 3,445 meters (11,302 feet). Emi Koussi is not only the tallest mountain in the Sahara but also one of the most prominent volcanic features in the region. The Tibesti Mountains are of volcanic origin, with numerous craters, lava flows, and geothermal features that give the landscape an otherworldly appearance.

Like the Ahaggar range, the Tibesti Mountains offer a refuge for both wildlife and human populations in the otherwise inhospitable Sahara. The mountains receive more rainfall than the surrounding desert, and their higher altitudes provide cooler temperatures, allowing a variety of plant and animal species to thrive. The range is home to animals such as Barbary sheep, rock hyraxes, and a variety of bird species, including vultures and eagles. The isolated valleys and canyons of the Tibesti also support pockets of vegetation, including acacia trees, tamarisks, and desert grasses, which provide food and shelter for the local wildlife.

The Tibesti Mountains have long been inhabited by the Toubou people, a nomadic group who have lived in the region for centuries. The Toubou are skilled navigators of the desert, and their knowledge of the Tibesti's rugged terrain has allowed them to survive in one of the most remote and difficult environments on Earth. The Toubou have traditionally relied on livestock herding and trade for their livelihoods, and their culture is closely tied to the mountains and the desert. The Tibesti Mountains are also rich in rock art, with numerous petroglyphs and cave paintings that date back thousands of years. These ancient artworks depict scenes of hunting, animals, and human figures, offering a glimpse into the lives of the early inhabitants of the region.

Further to the east, in the central Sahara, lies the Ennedi Plateau, a stunning and remote area of sandstone cliffs and rock formations located in northeastern Chad. The Ennedi Plateau is renowned for its unique and dramatic landscape, which includes natural arches, deep gorges, and towering rock spires that rise from the desert floor. The plateau is often referred to as a "Saharan Eden" due to its relative abundance of water sources, including springs and seasonal rivers, which have allowed life to flourish in this otherwise arid region. The Ennedi Plateau is home to a variety of plant and animal species, including crocodiles that live in some of the more permanent waterholes, a rare sight in the Sahara. The crocodiles are believed to be a relic population, left over from a time when the Sahara was much wetter and supported larger bodies of water.

The Ennedi Plateau is also famous for its rich collection of prehistoric rock art, which is some of the most extensive and well-preserved in the Sahara. The rock art of the Ennedi depicts a wide range of scenes, including images of animals such as giraffes, elephants, and cattle, as well as human figures engaged in activities like hunting, dancing, and herding. These artworks provide valuable insights into the lives of the people who lived in the region thousands of years ago when the Sahara was a more hospitable environment with ample water and vegetation. The Ennedi Plateau is now a UNESCO World Heritage Site, recognized for its cultural and natural significance, and it continues to attract archaeologists and adventurers alike.

In addition to the Ahaggar, Tibesti, and Ennedi ranges, there are several other notable mountain systems scattered throughout the Sahara, each with its own unique features and history. The Aïr Mountains in northern Niger, for example, are a series of ancient volcanic peaks and rocky plateaus that rise abruptly from the desert floor. The Aïr Mountains are known for their dramatic landscapes, including jagged peaks, deep canyons, and lush oases that support a variety of plant and animal life. The region has been inhabited for thousands of years, and the mountains are home to several important archaeological sites, including ancient tombs, rock carvings, and ruined settlements.

One of the most remarkable aspects of the Aïr Mountains is their role as a refuge for biodiversity in the otherwise harsh desert environment. The higher elevations of the Aïr range support pockets of vegetation, including acacia trees, date palms, and grasses, which provide food and shelter for animals such as gazelles, hyenas, and cheetahs. The mountains are also home to several species of birds, including raptors and migratory species that use the range as a stopover point during their long journeys across the desert. The Aïr Mountains are also an important cultural center for the Tuareg people, who have lived in the region for centuries and continue to practice their traditional way of life.

The geology of the Sahara's mountain ranges offers a window into the desert's ancient past. The formation of these mountains, which date back millions of years, is tied to the tectonic activity that shaped the African continent. Some of the ranges, like the Ahaggar and Tibesti, are the result of volcanic activity, while others, like the Aïr Mountains, are composed of ancient metamorphic and sedimentary rocks. The presence of these mountain ranges in the Sahara is a reminder that the desert is a dynamic and ever-changing landscape, shaped by powerful geological forces over the course of millions of years.

Despite their remote and often inaccessible locations, the hidden mountains of the Sahara have long attracted the attention of explorers, scientists, and adventurers. In recent years, advances in satellite imagery and aerial photography have revealed new insights into the geology and ecology of these mountain ranges, uncovering previously unknown features and helping to map the desert's rugged terrain. However, much of the Sahara's mountainous regions remain largely unexplored, and they continue to hold many secrets waiting to be discovered.

In conclusion, the hidden mountains of the Sahara Desert are a testament to the diversity and complexity of this vast desert landscape. Far from being a featureless expanse of sand, the Sahara is home to a range of towering peaks and rugged plateaus that provide shelter for a surprising array of life and have played an important role in the history of human civilization. From the volcanic craters of the Tibesti to the rock art of the Ennedi and the sacred peaks of the Ahaggar, these mountains are not only geological wonders but also cultural and ecological treasures. They remind us that even in the most extreme environments, life finds a way to persist and thrive.

Chapter 15: Camels: Ships of the Sahara Desert

Camels, often referred to as the "ships of the desert," are not only iconic symbols of the Sahara but also essential to the survival of both humans and animals in the vast, arid expanse of the world's largest hot desert. Their ability to traverse the seemingly endless dunes of the Sahara with ease and endurance has made them invaluable for millennia, especially to the nomadic peoples and traders who have depended on them for transportation, food, and companionship. The term "ships of the desert" is particularly fitting, as camels move with a steady, rocking motion across the sand, much like a boat on the ocean. Their unique physiology and adaptations have enabled them to withstand the Sahara's extreme conditions, earning them a central role in the history, economy, and culture of the desert.

Camels are specially adapted to survive the harsh conditions of the Sahara Desert, which is characterized by scorching heat during the day, freezing cold at night, and long stretches of time without any water. The most common species of camel in the Sahara is the dromedary camel, also known as the Arabian camel, which has one hump. This hump is not filled with water, as many believe, but with fat, which the camel uses as a reserve of energy. When food and water are scarce, the camel can metabolize the fat in its hump to provide sustenance. This allows camels to survive for long periods without eating or drinking, sometimes going for weeks without water. The hump also helps to regulate the camel's body temperature by reducing heat absorption into the rest of its body, making it easier for the animal to stay cool in the desert heat.

One of the camel's most remarkable adaptations is its ability to withstand extreme dehydration. Unlike most mammals, which can only lose a small percentage of their body weight in water before becoming severely dehydrated, camels can lose up to 25% of their body weight in water and still survive. When they do find water, they are capable of drinking up to 40 gallons in one go, rapidly replenishing their water stores. Their bodies are highly efficient at retaining water, with their kidneys and intestines adapted to conserve as much fluid as possible. Camels produce very concentrated urine and dry feces, which minimizes water loss. Their red blood cells are oval-shaped, allowing them to flow more easily in a dehydrated state and to withstand significant changes in blood viscosity when the animal rehydrates.

In addition to their ability to conserve water, camels have evolved several other physical traits that allow them to thrive in the Sahara's extreme environment. Their thick, woolly coats insulate them from the intense heat of the day and the cold of the night. The coat also helps reduce water loss through evaporation. Unlike most animals, camels can allow their body temperature to fluctuate throughout the day, rising during the hottest part of the day to avoid sweating and dropping at night when the desert cools down. This ability to tolerate a wide range of body temperatures reduces the amount of water they need to cool their bodies through sweating.

Camels' feet are another key adaptation that allows them to move efficiently through the Sahara's challenging terrain. Their large, padded feet are perfectly suited for walking on sand, as they distribute the animal's weight over a larger surface area, preventing them from sinking into the soft ground. This is particularly important in the vast stretches of sand dunes that cover much of the Sahara. The camel's feet are also designed to grip rocky surfaces, making them equally adept at crossing the desert's mountainous regions and rocky plains. The flexibility and durability of their feet ensure that camels can travel long distances across different types of terrain without injury or fatigue.

One of the most striking features of camels is their ability to protect themselves from the harsh desert environment. Their long, bushy eyelashes and thin, slit-like nostrils can close tightly to keep out sand and dust during the frequent sandstorms that sweep across the Sahara. Their thick lips allow them to eat thorny desert plants, which would be harmful to other animals. Camels' mouths are lined with tough, leathery tissue that enables them to chew tough, fibrous plants without injury. This dietary flexibility is crucial in the desert, where food sources can be scarce and unpredictable.

For thousands of years, camels have played a central role in the lives of the people who inhabit the Sahara. The domestication of camels, which is believed to have occurred around 3,000 years ago in the Arabian Peninsula, transformed life in the desert by enabling long-distance travel and trade. Camels became the backbone of the trans-Saharan trade routes, which connected North Africa to sub-Saharan Africa, the Middle East, and beyond. These trade routes facilitated the exchange of goods such as gold, salt, ivory, spices, textiles, and slaves, and they helped spread cultures, languages, and religions across vast distances. The camel caravans that crossed the Sahara could travel for weeks or even months, covering thousands of miles. A typical caravan would consist of hundreds of camels, each loaded with goods to be traded, as well as water and food supplies for the journey.

The importance of camels in trans-Saharan trade cannot be overstated. The ability to transport large quantities of goods over long distances without needing to stop frequently for water or rest made camels the most reliable and efficient means of transportation in the desert. The camels were loaded with sacks of salt, often weighing as much as 200 pounds, which was a highly valuable commodity in the ancient world. Salt, which was essential for preserving food and maintaining health, was mined in places like the Taoudenni salt mines in present-day Mali and transported by camel to trading centers such as Timbuktu, where it was exchanged for gold and other goods.

The camel's role in facilitating trade was so important that entire cities and empires in the Sahara and Sahel regions grew wealthy and powerful as a result of the camel caravans. Cities such as Timbuktu,

Gao, and Agadez became major centers of commerce, learning, and culture due to their strategic positions along the trans-Saharan trade routes. The wealth generated by the trade in gold, salt, and other goods helped to build monumental architecture, fund universities and libraries, and foster the spread of Islam throughout North and West Africa. The camel, as the primary mode of transport across the Sahara, was at the heart of this economic and cultural transformation.

Beyond their role in trade, camels have been crucial to the survival of nomadic peoples who have lived in the Sahara for centuries, such as the Tuareg, Bedouin, and Berber groups. For these desert-dwelling communities, camels provide not only transportation but also food, clothing, and shelter. Camel milk, which is highly nutritious and rich in vitamins, minerals, and proteins, is a staple food for many nomadic groups. It is especially important in the desert, where other sources of nutrition are often scarce. Camel milk can be consumed fresh, fermented into yogurt, or churned into butter. It is considered a lifeline in the harsh desert environment, providing hydration and nourishment during long journeys.

Camel meat is another important source of food for nomadic peoples in the Sahara. The meat is lean and rich in protein, and it is often preserved through drying or smoking, allowing it to be stored for long periods in the desert's hot climate. In addition to their milk and meat, camels provide wool, which is used to make clothing, blankets, and tents. Camel hair is highly prized for its durability and insulating properties, making it ideal for protecting against the extremes of desert temperatures. The nomads also use camels' hides to make leather goods, including saddles, bags, and footwear.

The close relationship between camels and the nomadic peoples of the Sahara goes beyond the practical; it is also deeply cultural. Camels are revered in many Saharan societies, where they are often seen as symbols of wealth, status, and resilience. In Tuareg culture, for example, a man's wealth is traditionally measured by the number of camels he owns, and camels play a prominent role in Tuareg weddings, festivals, and other social rituals. Camel races and camel beauty contests are also popular in many desert communities, where the strength, speed, and appearance of the animals are celebrated.

In modern times, the role of camels in the Sahara has shifted somewhat due to changes in transportation, trade, and technology. The development of motorized vehicles, airplanes, and more modern infrastructure has reduced the reliance on camels for long-distance travel and trade. However, camels remain an important part of the culture and economy of the Sahara, particularly in rural and nomadic communities. Tourism has also emerged as a significant industry in some parts of the Sahara, with camels playing a key role in desert tours and expeditions. Tourists are often eager to experience the desert by riding camels, as it offers a connection to the ancient traditions of Saharan travel and a unique way to explore the landscape.

Camel treks across the Sahara are now a popular attraction, allowing visitors to experience the desert in much the same way as traders and nomads have for centuries. These treks, often led by experienced guides from nomadic communities, provide a glimpse into the traditional way of life in the desert, as well as an opportunity to appreciate the incredible adaptations of the camel to the harsh desert environment. The slow, rhythmic pace of a camel journey offers a sense of peace and connection with the vastness of the Sahara, allowing travelers to immerse themselves in the beauty and solitude of the desert.

In addition to their continued role in tourism and local economies, camels are also increasingly recognized for their environmental sustainability. As concerns about climate change and desertification grow, camels are being seen as a valuable resource for sustainable agriculture in arid regions. Their ability to thrive on sparse vegetation and to survive in areas with little water makes them well-suited to environments that are becoming increasingly inhospitable due to climate change. In some regions, camel farming is being promoted as a sustainable alternative to more water-intensive livestock, such as cattle, which are less adapted to dry environments.

In conclusion, camels truly are the "ships of the Sahara," indispensable to the history, culture, and survival of the people who inhabit this vast desert. Their remarkable adaptations to the extreme conditions of the Sahara have allowed them to thrive in one of the harshest environments on Earth, and their role in trade, transportation, and daily life has shaped the development of civilizations across the desert for thousands of years. Even in the modern world, camels continue to play a vital role in the economy and culture of the Sahara, symbolizing resilience, endurance, and the unique relationship between humans and animals in this extraordinary environment.

Chapter 16: Life in the Sahara's Remote Villages

Life in the remote villages of the Sahara Desert is a story of resilience, adaptation, and an intimate relationship with one of the harshest environments on Earth. These villages, often small and scattered across the vast desert, are home to people who have lived in this region for centuries, carrying on traditions passed down through generations. The Sahara's villages are unique in their ability to maintain a sense of community, culture, and survival in the face of extreme heat, scarcity of resources, and isolation. Each village has its own way of life, deeply influenced by its geographic location, access to water, and cultural heritage, but they all share common challenges and solutions shaped by the desert.

Water, the most precious resource in the Sahara, dictates the very existence of these villages. Life revolves around the availability of water sources, and many villages are built near oases, where underground aquifers provide a steady, albeit limited, supply of water. These oases serve as lifelines for both humans and animals. The presence of water allows for the cultivation of crops such as date palms, barley, and millet, which form the staple diet of the village inhabitants. Date palms, in particular, are of immense importance, not only as a food source but also for their leaves, which are used for making baskets, mats, and other household items. The shade provided by these trees also helps create a more habitable microclimate within the village, shielding inhabitants from the direct heat of the sun.

Villagers have developed ingenious methods to conserve and manage water, often using ancient techniques that have been passed down for generations. One such method is the foggara or qanat system, an underground network of tunnels that channel water from distant sources to the village. These systems help minimize evaporation in the searing heat and ensure a consistent water supply for irrigation and drinking. Wells are another common feature in Sahara villages, though they often require villagers to dig deep into the earth to reach water. Maintaining and repairing these water systems is a communal task, with everyone in the village contributing to their upkeep.

Agriculture in these villages is often limited to small-scale subsistence farming, as the extreme climate and lack of water make large-scale farming impossible. Farmers rely on traditional methods, such as terrace farming, to maximize the use of available water and protect the soil from erosion. Livestock, particularly goats, sheep, and camels, are also vital to the villagers' way of life. These animals provide milk, meat, wool, and leather, which are essential for daily survival and also serve as a form of wealth. Camels, in particular, play a crucial role in the transportation of goods, allowing villagers to trade with other settlements or to travel across the desert when necessary.

The economy of these remote villages is largely based on a combination of agriculture, animal husbandry, and small-scale trade. Markets, though rare and often far away, are vital hubs where villagers can sell their produce, buy necessary supplies, and exchange news and ideas with people from other villages. Some villages are located along ancient trade routes, and while modern transportation has changed the way goods move across the Sahara, remnants of this history remain in the trading practices and relationships between different communities. Handicrafts, such as woven textiles, pottery, and metalwork, are also important sources of income for many villagers. These crafts are often made using traditional techniques and are sold in local markets or to tourists who venture into the desert.

Life in these remote villages is deeply influenced by the cultural traditions and beliefs of the people who live there. Many of the inhabitants are from nomadic or semi-nomadic backgrounds, such as the Tuareg, Berber, and Bedouin peoples. While some have settled permanently in villages, their nomadic heritage still shapes their way of life. Hospitality is a core value in these communities, and it is not uncommon for travelers, whether they are fellow villagers, traders, or tourists, to be welcomed with tea and offered a place to stay. This tradition of hospitality is rooted in the harsh realities of desert life, where mutual aid and generosity are often necessary for survival.

Religion also plays a central role in the daily lives of the villagers. Islam is the predominant religion in the Sahara, and the rhythm of life in many villages is structured around the five daily prayers. Mosques, often simple structures made of mud and clay, serve as the spiritual and social centers of the village. Religious festivals, such as Ramadan and Eid, are important events that bring the community together for prayer, feasting, and celebration. These festivals provide a welcome break from the rigors of daily life and reinforce the bonds of community and faith.

Education in the remote villages of the Sahara is often limited, especially in the more isolated settlements. Schools, when they exist, are typically small and understaffed, with few resources. However, many villages prioritize the education of their children, understanding that knowledge can provide opportunities beyond the confines of the desert. In some cases, nomadic schools travel with the children of nomadic families, allowing them to receive an education even as they move from place to place in search of grazing land for their animals. For those who live in permanent villages, education often focuses on both religious and practical subjects, teaching children the Quran alongside essential skills like farming, animal husbandry, and traditional crafts.

Health care in these remote villages is another challenge. Medical facilities are often far away, and access to modern healthcare is limited. Traditional medicine, passed down through generations, is commonly used to treat illnesses and injuries. Herbal remedies, often made from desert plants, are a crucial part of the villagers' health care practices. However, for serious illnesses or injuries, villagers must often travel long distances to reach the nearest clinic or hospital. This lack of medical infrastructure contributes to high rates of infant mortality and a lower life expectancy compared to urban areas.

Despite the challenges, there is a strong sense of community in these villages. People rely on each other for support, whether it's sharing food and water, helping to repair homes, or caring for the sick and elderly. Family ties are incredibly important, and extended families often live close to one another, providing a built-in support system. The village itself functions as a tight-knit community where everyone knows each other, and decisions are often made collectively, with elders playing a significant role in guiding and advising the younger generations.

The architecture of these villages is another testament to human ingenuity and adaptation to the desert environment. Houses are typically made from mud bricks, clay, or stone, materials that are readily available and provide insulation from the extreme temperatures. The thick walls of these homes help keep the interior cool during the day and warm at night, while flat roofs allow rainwater to be collected and stored for later use. In some villages, the houses are built close together, creating narrow, shaded streets that help reduce the heat and create a more pleasant living environment. The design of these villages is a reflection of the deep understanding the inhabitants have of their environment and their ability to build sustainably with limited resources.

In recent years, the encroachment of modernity has begun to change life in some of these remote villages. Solar power is increasingly being used to generate electricity, providing villagers with access to lighting, communication, and even refrigeration. Mobile phones, though not ubiquitous, have become more common, allowing villagers to stay in touch with relatives in other parts of the desert or in distant cities. These technological advancements have made life in the Sahara's villages somewhat easier, but they have also brought new challenges, as younger generations are increasingly drawn to the cities in search of education, jobs, and a more modern lifestyle.

Climate change is another factor that is having an impact on life in the Sahara's remote villages. Rising temperatures and changing rainfall patterns are making the desert even more inhospitable, leading to increased desertification and the depletion of already scarce water resources. Many villagers are finding it harder to sustain their traditional ways of life, as their crops fail and their livestock struggle to find enough food and water. Some villages are being abandoned altogether as people are forced to move to more hospitable areas or to urban centers in search of better opportunities. The challenges posed by climate change are profound, and they threaten not only the survival of these villages but also the rich cultural heritage they represent.

Despite these challenges, there is a deep sense of pride and identity among the people who live in the Sahara's remote villages. Their way of life is deeply connected to the land, and many villagers see themselves as custodians of the desert, responsible for preserving its delicate ecosystems and its traditions. The Sahara may be harsh and unforgiving, but it is also a place of beauty and mystery, and those who call it home have developed a profound respect for its power and its rhythms. Life in the Sahara's villages may be difficult, but it is also rich with meaning, connection, and a sense of purpose that comes from living in harmony with one of the most extreme environments on the planet.

In conclusion, life in the remote villages of the Sahara Desert is a testament to human endurance, creativity, and the ability to adapt to the most challenging circumstances. These villages, often isolated from the rest of the world, have developed unique ways of surviving and thriving in an environment where resources are scarce and the climate is unforgiving. The villagers' strong sense of community, their deep knowledge of the land, and their ability to blend tradition with modernity ensure that, despite the many challenges they face, the way of life in these remote corners of the Sahara will continue to endure for generations to come.

Chapter 17: The Sahara's Impact on Global Climate

The Sahara Desert, the largest hot desert in the world, plays a significant and far-reaching role in shaping global climate patterns. Its sheer size and location in northern Africa, covering an area of about 9.2 million square kilometers, makes it a powerful force that influences weather systems far beyond its borders. The Sahara's impact on the global climate is not just confined to its immediate surroundings but extends across continents, affecting everything from wind patterns and rainfall to ocean currents and atmospheric circulation. Its influence is complex and multifaceted, with both direct and indirect effects that scientists are continually working to understand. Despite being one of the harshest environments on Earth, the Sahara has a profound and lasting impact on the planet's climate.

One of the most prominent ways the Sahara influences global climate is through its role as a massive heat engine. During the day, the desert absorbs vast amounts of solar radiation, making it one of the hottest places on Earth. The intense heat generated by the sun warms the surface of the desert, creating powerful updrafts of hot air that rise high into the atmosphere. This hot air is carried by the wind, contributing to the formation of high-pressure systems over the desert. These high-pressure zones have a stabilizing effect on the atmosphere, suppressing cloud formation and reducing the likelihood of precipitation, not just over the Sahara itself, but also in regions downwind of the desert.

The Sahara's high-pressure systems are a key driver of some of the most significant weather patterns on the planet, including the trade winds, which are crucial for global atmospheric circulation. The trade winds, which blow from the east to the west across the tropics, are partly driven by the temperature differences between the hot desert and the cooler regions surrounding it. These winds are not only important for transporting moisture and heat across the globe but also for the development of weather systems, including tropical storms and hurricanes. The Sahara's influence on the trade winds means that it plays a role in determining the weather in faraway places, such as the Caribbean, Central America, and even the southern United States.

Another major impact of the Sahara on global climate is through the production and dispersal of dust. The Sahara is one of the largest sources of airborne dust in the world, with massive amounts of fine particles being lifted into the atmosphere by strong winds. Each year, it is estimated that between 60 to 200 million tons of Sahara dust is carried across the Atlantic Ocean by the trade winds, a phenomenon known as the Saharan Air Layer. This dust travels thousands of kilometers, affecting air quality, weather patterns, and ecosystems across the globe. The Saharan dust has a significant impact on the climate, both regionally and globally.

One of the most direct effects of Saharan dust is its influence on the formation and intensity of hurricanes in the Atlantic Ocean. The dry, dusty air from the Sahara can suppress the development of tropical storms by introducing a layer of dry, stable air into the atmosphere, which inhibits the upward motion of moist air that fuels hurricanes. This can lead to fewer or weaker hurricanes during the Atlantic hurricane season. On the other hand, in certain conditions, the same dust can contribute to the development of more intense storms by altering the temperature structure of the atmosphere. This dual role of Sahara dust in hurricane formation highlights the complex ways in which the desert interacts with weather systems across the globe.

Saharan dust also plays an important role in the global carbon cycle and the health of marine and terrestrial ecosystems. When the dust is carried across the Atlantic and deposited in the Amazon rainforest, it provides essential nutrients, such as phosphorus and iron, which help fertilize the soil and support plant growth. The Amazon Basin, often referred to as the "lungs of the Earth," is crucial for absorbing large amounts of carbon dioxide and regulating the planet's climate. Without the nutrients provided by Saharan dust, the Amazon's ability to absorb carbon would be significantly reduced, impacting its role as a critical carbon sink. Similarly, when Saharan dust settles over the oceans, it can fertilize phytoplankton, tiny marine organisms that are essential for carbon sequestration. These microscopic plants absorb carbon dioxide from the atmosphere and play a vital role in regulating global climate by helping to reduce greenhouse gas levels.

The Sahara's dust also has a profound impact on air quality and human health. When large dust storms occur, they can carry particles across continents, affecting regions as far away as Europe and North America. These dust particles can cause respiratory problems, particularly for people with asthma or other lung conditions. The dust can also affect visibility and create hazardous conditions for transportation, particularly in regions downwind of the Sahara, such as the Mediterranean and the Canary Islands. In recent years, the frequency and intensity of dust storms have increased, likely due to a combination of climate change and land-use practices that have disturbed the desert's surface.

In addition to its influence on weather patterns, the Sahara Desert also plays a key role in the African monsoon system, which brings seasonal rains to much of West and Central Africa. The extreme heat generated by the Sahara during the summer months creates a low-pressure zone over the desert, which pulls in moist air from the Atlantic Ocean. This moisture-laden air travels inland, eventually leading to the onset of the West African monsoon. The monsoon is essential for agriculture and water supplies in many African countries, but the timing and intensity of the rains can vary dramatically from year to year, partly due to the influence of the Sahara. Changes in the desert's temperature and dust production can alter the strength and location of the monsoon, leading to droughts in some years and flooding in others.

The interaction between the Sahara Desert and the African monsoon system also has implications for global climate patterns. The monsoon's strength can influence the position of the Intertropical Convergence Zone (ITCZ), a band of clouds that encircles the Earth near the equator and is responsible for much of the planet's tropical rainfall. When the Sahara is hotter, the ITCZ can shift farther north, bringing more rain to the Sahel region, which lies just south of the Sahara. Conversely, when the desert is cooler, the ITCZ shifts southward, leading to droughts in the Sahel. These shifts in rainfall patterns can have ripple effects across the globe, affecting everything from agricultural production in Africa to weather patterns in the Americas and Asia.

Over geological timescales, the Sahara has undergone dramatic shifts in climate, oscillating between periods of extreme aridity and more temperate conditions. During the wet phases, known as the "Green Sahara" or "African Humid Periods," the desert was covered in grasslands, lakes, and rivers, and supported a rich diversity of plant and animal life. These periods were driven by changes in the Earth's orbit, which altered the amount of solar radiation reaching the Northern Hemisphere and, in turn, the strength of the African monsoon. During these humid periods, the Sahara acted as a carbon sink, absorbing carbon dioxide from the atmosphere through increased vegetation. However, as the Earth's orbit shifted again, the Sahara returned to its current arid state, becoming a source of carbon as plant life disappeared and the desert expanded.

The Sahara's role in global climate is further complicated by human activity. Deforestation, overgrazing, and agricultural practices in regions bordering the Sahara, particularly in the Sahel, have contributed to desertification, the process by which fertile land becomes desert. This human-induced expansion of the Sahara exacerbates the desert's impact on global climate by increasing dust production, altering wind patterns, and reducing the land's ability to absorb carbon. Climate change is also expected to increase the frequency and intensity of heatwaves in the Sahara, further amplifying the desert's influence on global weather patterns.

In recent years, scientists have begun exploring the possibility of using the Sahara as a site for large-scale renewable energy projects, particularly solar power. The desert's vast, open spaces and intense sunlight make it an ideal location for solar farms, which could generate enough electricity to power entire regions. If such projects were implemented on a large scale, they could help reduce global reliance on fossil fuels and mitigate the effects of climate change. However, these projects would also have the potential to alter the local and global climate in unexpected ways. For example, the large-scale deployment of solar panels could reduce the amount of sunlight reflected back into the atmosphere by the desert's bright surface, potentially altering temperature and wind patterns.

In conclusion, the Sahara Desert's impact on global climate is vast and multifaceted. From its role as a heat engine driving atmospheric circulation to its production of dust that fertilizes ecosystems and influences weather patterns, the Sahara has far-reaching effects on the planet's climate system. Its interactions with the African monsoon and the ITCZ, as well as its influence on hurricane formation and the global carbon cycle, make it a critical player in both regional and global climate dynamics. As climate change continues to reshape the planet, understanding the Sahara's complex role in the global climate system will be essential for predicting and mitigating the effects of a warming world.

Chapter 18: The Salt Trade Routes of the Sahara

The salt trade routes of the Sahara Desert are a fascinating chapter in human history, illustrating the ingenuity and resilience of ancient traders who traversed one of the most inhospitable environments on Earth. These routes, which connected North Africa to West Africa, were essential for the exchange of goods, cultures, and ideas across vast distances. Salt, a precious and vital commodity, played a central role in these trade networks. Despite the harsh desert conditions, the salt trade thrived for centuries, shaping the economies and societies of the regions it touched. The salt trade routes were more than just pathways for exchanging goods—they were lifelines for the people who depended on the trade for their survival and prosperity.

Salt was one of the most valuable commodities in the ancient world, particularly in regions like West Africa, where it was scarce. In a time before refrigeration, salt was essential for preserving food, particularly meat, making it crucial for both everyday sustenance and long-term storage. It was also important for human health, as salt helps regulate bodily functions and maintain hydration, especially in hot climates like those found in West Africa. The demand for salt in these regions was immense, and the Sahara's vast salt deposits became the key to meeting this demand.

The primary sources of salt in the Sahara were the great salt mines of the desert, particularly in places like Taghaza, Bilma, and Taoudenni. These mines produced vast quantities of rock salt, which was extracted from the earth and shaped into slabs for transport. The extraction of salt was labor-intensive and often carried out by enslaved workers, particularly in the case of the Taoudenni mines in modern-day Mali, where salt mining continues to this day. These slabs of salt, sometimes referred to as "salt cakes" or "salt bars," became a form of currency in the trade networks, their value determined by their weight and size.

The journey from the salt mines to the trading centers of West Africa was long and perilous. Traders, known as "salt caravans," had to traverse the vast expanse of the Sahara, facing extreme heat during the day and freezing temperatures at night, along with the constant threat of sandstorms, dehydration, and exhaustion. The caravans relied heavily on camels, often referred to as the "ships of the desert," to carry their heavy loads of salt across the desert. Camels were ideally suited for this task due to their ability to endure long periods without water and their capacity to carry substantial loads. A typical salt caravan could consist of hundreds or even thousands of camels, each carrying several slabs of salt, which could weigh up to 90 kilograms (200 pounds) per slab.

The salt caravans traveled along well-established trade routes, many of which had been in use for centuries or even millennia. These routes connected the northern Saharan regions with the bustling trading cities of West Africa, such as Timbuktu, Gao, and Djenne. These cities, located along the Niger River and its tributaries, were vibrant centers of commerce and culture, serving as key points of exchange not only for salt but also for gold, ivory, slaves, textiles, and other goods. Timbuktu, in particular, became legendary as a hub of wealth and knowledge, attracting scholars and merchants from across the Islamic world and beyond.

The salt trade was deeply intertwined with the gold trade, which was equally important in West Africa. The gold fields of the region, particularly in modern-day Mali and Ghana, were some of the richest in the world during the medieval period. Gold was in high demand in North Africa and Europe, where it was used for coinage, jewelry, and religious artifacts. The salt-gold trade became the backbone of the trans-Saharan economy, with North African traders bringing salt to West Africa and returning with gold. This exchange was so lucrative that it helped to build powerful empires in West Africa, such as the

Ghana Empire, the Mali Empire, and the Songhai Empire, which controlled key parts of the trade routes and taxed the goods that passed through their territories.

The salt trade routes were not just conduits for economic exchange; they were also important channels for cultural and intellectual exchange. The traders who traversed the desert brought with them not only goods but also ideas, stories, and religious beliefs. Islam, which had spread across North Africa by the 7th century, was introduced to West Africa through the trans-Saharan trade routes. Muslim traders and scholars played a key role in the Islamization of the region, particularly in the cities of Timbuktu, Gao, and Djenne, where Islamic learning and culture flourished. Timbuktu, in particular, became a renowned center of Islamic scholarship, with its famous libraries and universities attracting students and scholars from across the Muslim world.

The spread of Islam through the salt trade routes had a profound impact on the societies of West Africa. It helped to unify the region under a common religious and legal framework, facilitating trade and diplomacy between different peoples and cultures. Islamic law, or sharia, provided a set of principles for conducting trade, ensuring fairness and trust between traders from different regions. The adoption of Islam also helped to integrate West Africa into the wider Islamic world, opening up new opportunities for trade, education, and cultural exchange.

Despite its importance, the salt trade was fraught with danger. The Sahara is one of the most hostile environments on Earth, and crossing it required careful planning and expertise. The desert's vastness, combined with its extreme temperatures and lack of water, meant that traders were always at risk of running out of supplies or losing their way. Caravans had to follow specific routes where they could find water at oases or wells, which were often located far apart. Even a small mistake, such as taking the wrong turn or misjudging the amount of water needed for the journey, could lead to disaster. Sandstorms, which could appear suddenly and with great ferocity, were another constant threat, capable of burying entire caravans under shifting dunes.

In addition to the natural hazards of the desert, traders also had to contend with the threat of banditry. The wealth carried by the salt caravans made them prime targets for raiders, who would attack the caravans in hopes of seizing their valuable cargo. To protect themselves, caravans often traveled in large groups, and some even hired armed guards to fend off potential attackers. The threat of violence was particularly high in politically unstable regions, where local rulers could not guarantee the safety of the trade routes.

The decline of the trans-Saharan salt trade began in the 15th and 16th centuries, as European maritime powers, such as Portugal and Spain, began exploring alternative trade routes along the West African coast. These sea routes allowed for the direct exchange of goods between Europe and West Africa, bypassing the need for the arduous desert crossings. The rise of European colonialism and the exploitation of West African resources by European powers further weakened the traditional trade networks. The discovery of new sources of salt and gold outside the Sahara also diminished the importance of the desert trade routes.

Despite its decline, the legacy of the salt trade routes remains deeply embedded in the history and culture of the Sahara and West Africa. Many of the old trade routes are still used today, though the goods being transported have changed. Salt mining continues in some parts of the Sahara, particularly in places like Taoudenni, where traditional methods of extraction and transport have been preserved. The salt caravans, though fewer in number, still make their long journeys across the desert, a living link to a bygone era of trans-Saharan trade.

In addition to its economic and cultural legacy, the salt trade routes of the Sahara have left a lasting impact on the geography and infrastructure of the region. Many of the ancient trading cities, such as Timbuktu and Gao, remain important cultural and historical landmarks, though they have lost much of their former economic significance. The routes themselves, though no longer as vital as they once were, have shaped the settlement patterns and development of the regions they connected. In many ways, the salt trade helped to create the political and cultural landscape of the Sahara and West Africa, leaving behind a legacy that continues to influence the region today.

In conclusion, the salt trade routes of the Sahara Desert were more than just pathways for the exchange of goods; they were arteries of civilization, connecting distant peoples and cultures across one of the harshest environments on Earth. The trade in salt, a seemingly simple commodity, was the foundation of powerful empires and flourishing cities, driving economic, cultural, and intellectual exchange across vast distances. The traders who braved the desert not only transported goods but also ideas, religion, and knowledge, helping to shape the history of both North and West Africa. Though the salt trade has declined, its legacy endures in the cultural and historical fabric of the Sahara and beyond, a testament to the enduring power of human ingenuity and resilience in the face of adversity.

Chapter 19: Ancient Fossils in the Sahara Desert

The Sahara Desert, while known today as a vast, arid expanse of sand and rock, holds an extraordinary secret beneath its surface: it is one of the richest regions in the world for discovering ancient fossils. These fossils tell the story of a time when the Sahara was not a desert at all, but a lush, vibrant landscape teeming with life. Stretching back hundreds of millions of years, the fossil record of the Sahara provides invaluable insights into the evolution of life on Earth, as well as the dramatic climatic and geological changes that have shaped the region over time. From the remains of prehistoric sea creatures to the fossils of enormous dinosaurs and early human ancestors, the Sahara is a treasure trove for paleontologists and scientists studying Earth's ancient history.

Long before the Sahara became the parched desert it is today, it was part of a tropical region that experienced much wetter and more temperate climates. During the Paleozoic and Mesozoic eras, roughly between 500 million and 65 million years ago, large portions of what is now the Sahara were covered by vast oceans, rivers, and lush vegetation. These environments supported a diverse range of life forms, many of which have been preserved as fossils in the rock layers beneath the desert's sands. One of the most fascinating aspects of the Sahara's fossil record is its richness in marine fossils, which provide evidence of ancient seas that once covered the region.

One of the key periods of interest in the Sahara's fossil history is the Cretaceous period, which lasted from about 145 million to 66 million years ago. During this time, much of the Sahara was submerged beneath the Tethys Sea, a vast body of water that connected what is now the Mediterranean Sea with the Indian Ocean. The presence of this ancient sea is evident in the abundance of marine fossils found in the Sahara, including the remains of ammonites, ancient cephalopods with spiral shells, and plesiosaurs, large marine reptiles that dominated the seas. Fossils of these creatures have been discovered in many parts of the Sahara, particularly in regions like Morocco, which has become a hotspot for fossil hunting.

One of the most significant discoveries in the Sahara's fossil record is the remains of giant predatory fish and other marine megafauna that lived during the Cretaceous period. In particular, the fossilized remains of a creature known as *Carcharodontosaurus* have been found in the Sahara. This massive predator, which lived about 100 million years ago, was one of the largest carnivorous dinosaurs ever to roam the Earth. Its teeth, which resemble those of modern-day sharks, give this creature its name, which means "shark-toothed lizard." *Carcharodontosaurus* was a fearsome predator that hunted in the coastal regions of what is now the Sahara, preying on both marine and terrestrial animals.

In addition to marine reptiles and giant fish, the Sahara is also home to the fossils of dinosaurs that once roamed the land. One of the most famous dinosaur fossils discovered in the Sahara is that of *Spinosaurus*, a massive, sail-backed predator that lived around 100 million years ago. *Spinosaurus* was one of the largest carnivorous dinosaurs, even larger than the more famous *Tyrannosaurus rex*. What makes *Spinosaurus* particularly unique is its semi-aquatic lifestyle; fossil evidence suggests that it spent much of its time hunting in rivers and coastal waters, feeding on fish and other aquatic prey. The discovery of *Spinosaurus* fossils in the Sahara has provided paleontologists with valuable insights into the diversity of dinosaur species and their adaptations to different environments.

The Sahara's fossil record is not limited to large predators. Many herbivorous dinosaurs, such as *Ouranosaurus*, have also been found in the region. *Ouranosaurus* was a duck-billed dinosaur with a distinctive sail-like structure on its back, similar to that of *Spinosaurus*. It lived in the lush floodplains of the Sahara during the Cretaceous period, feeding on vegetation and likely using its sail to regulate its body temperature or attract mates. The discovery of such herbivores in the Sahara highlights the incredible diversity of life that once thrived in what is now a barren desert.

In addition to dinosaurs and marine reptiles, the Sahara has also yielded a wealth of fossilized remains of other ancient creatures, including early mammals, crocodiles, and turtles. One of the most notable discoveries in the Sahara is the fossil of *Sarcosuchus*, also known as the "SuperCroc." *Sarcosuchus* was a giant crocodile that lived during the Cretaceous period and grew up to 12 meters (40 feet) in length, making it one of the largest crocodiles ever to exist. Its fossilized remains have been found in various parts of the Sahara, particularly in Niger. This enormous predator likely hunted both in the water and on land, preying on dinosaurs and other large animals.

As fascinating as the fossil record of the Mesozoic era is, the Sahara's history does not end with the extinction of the dinosaurs. After the demise of the dinosaurs 66 million years ago, the region continued to evolve, and the fossil record provides evidence of the many changes that occurred in the millennia that followed. During the Paleogene and Neogene periods, which spanned from about 66 million to 2.6 million years ago, the Sahara underwent significant climatic shifts, transforming from a lush, green landscape into the arid desert we know today. The fossilized remains of plants, animals, and even early human ancestors from these periods offer a glimpse into how life adapted to these changes.

One of the most intriguing aspects of the Sahara's more recent fossil history is the discovery of hominid fossils, which shed light on the evolution of early humans. Fossil evidence suggests that the Sahara was once a thriving habitat for early human ancestors, particularly during the periods when the region was wetter and more hospitable. The discovery of ancient stone tools and fossilized remains of hominins, such as *Australopithecus* and *Homo erectus*, in parts of the

Sahara indicates that early humans lived and migrated through the region as they spread across Africa.

The Sahara's ancient fossils also include the remains of large mammals that lived during the Pleistocene epoch, which lasted from about 2.6 million to 11,700 years ago. During this time, the Sahara experienced several periods of increased rainfall, known as "Green Sahara" periods, during which the desert was transformed into a savannah-like landscape with abundant vegetation and wildlife. Fossils from these periods include the remains of elephants, giraffes, hippos, and other large herbivores, as well as the predators that hunted them, such as lions and hyenas. These fossils provide evidence of a time when the Sahara was a fertile region, supporting a rich diversity of life.

One of the most remarkable fossil sites in the Sahara is the Fayum Depression in Egypt, which has yielded a treasure trove of fossils from the Eocene epoch, about 56 to 34 million years ago. During this period, the Fayum region was a lush, swampy environment teeming with life, and the fossils found there include early ancestors of modern mammals, such as primates, bats, and whales. The Fayum fossils provide a unique window into the evolution of mammals during a critical period in Earth's history, and they have helped scientists trace the origins of many modern species.

In recent years, the study of Sahara fossils has been revolutionized by advances in technology, particularly in the field of paleontology. Techniques such as CT scanning and 3D imaging have allowed scientists to study fossils in greater detail than ever before, providing new insights into the anatomy, behavior, and ecology of ancient creatures. These technologies have also made it possible to study fossils that are still embedded in rock, allowing paleontologists to reconstruct entire skeletons and even create digital models of extinct species.

The discovery of fossils in the Sahara has not only provided valuable scientific knowledge but also sparked significant interest among the public. Fossil hunters and paleontologists from around the world have flocked to the region, hoping to uncover new specimens and contribute to our understanding of Earth's prehistoric past. However, the increasing commercialization of fossil collecting, particularly in countries like Morocco, has raised concerns about the preservation of these valuable scientific resources. Many fossils are sold to private collectors or on the black market, depriving scientists of the opportunity to study them in detail.

Despite these challenges, the study of ancient fossils in the Sahara continues to be a vibrant and important field of research. Each new discovery adds to our understanding of the region's rich and complex history, revealing the incredible diversity of life that once thrived in what is now the world's largest hot desert. As scientists continue to explore the Sahara's fossil record, they are uncovering new clues about the forces that have shaped our planet and the life forms that have inhabited it over the millennia.

In conclusion, the Sahara Desert is a repository of ancient fossils that tell the story of a world long past, when the region was home to oceans, rivers, and diverse ecosystems teeming with life. From marine reptiles and dinosaurs to early mammals and hominins, the fossils of the Sahara offer a unique window into Earth's evolutionary history. These fossils not only provide valuable scientific insights but also challenge our perceptions of the desert as a barren, lifeless place, reminding us that the Sahara was once a thriving, vibrant ecosystem. As research continues, the ancient fossils of the Sahara will undoubtedly continue to reveal new and exciting discoveries, deepening our understanding of the history of life on Earth.

Chapter 20: Modern Challenges Facing the Sahara Desert

The Sahara Desert, while vast and awe-inspiring, faces numerous modern challenges that threaten both the environment and the people who live there. Spanning approximately 9.2 million square kilometers across North Africa, the Sahara is the largest hot desert in the world, covering parts of 11 countries, including Algeria, Chad, Egypt, Libya, Mali, Mauritania, Morocco, Niger, Sudan, Tunisia, and Western Sahara. These modern challenges are not only environmental but also social, economic, and geopolitical, impacting millions of people and countless ecosystems.

One of the most pressing issues facing the Sahara Desert is desertification, a process where fertile land becomes increasingly arid and eventually turns into desert. Although desertification is a natural phenomenon that has occurred over thousands of years, human activities are accelerating the process at an alarming rate. Overgrazing by livestock, deforestation, unsustainable agricultural practices, and the overuse of water resources are all contributing factors. As populations grow and pressure on land increases, areas around the Sahara, particularly in the Sahel region to the south, are becoming more desert-like, pushing communities into greater vulnerability.

The Sahara has always had extreme weather, but climate change is intensifying these conditions, exacerbating the challenges faced by the region. Rising global temperatures are leading to longer and more intense heatwaves, while rainfall is becoming more erratic and unpredictable. In some areas, rainfall has decreased significantly, worsening drought conditions and making it even harder for vegetation to grow. This in turn accelerates desertification, as fewer plants mean less moisture in the soil, which contributes to the erosion of the land and the formation of sand dunes. For the people living in and around the Sahara, these climatic shifts are making agriculture, pastoralism, and even basic survival increasingly difficult.

Water scarcity is one of the most significant challenges in the Sahara, both for the environment and the human populations that depend on it. The Sahara is known for its lack of water, but many areas rely on underground aquifers and oases for their water needs. These precious water sources are now under threat due to over-extraction, population growth, and pollution. As people and livestock draw more water from underground aquifers, the levels of these reserves are depleting faster than they can naturally replenish. Additionally, some of these aquifers are fossil water, meaning that they were filled thousands of years ago when the climate was wetter and are not being replenished by modern rainfall. Once depleted, these ancient aquifers may never be restored, posing a dire threat to the sustainability of life in the Sahara.

Oases, the lifeblood of many Saharan communities, are also facing serious challenges. These isolated patches of greenery provide water and fertile land for agriculture, making them crucial for the survival of both people and wildlife in the desert. However, as water levels drop and temperatures rise, many oases are shrinking, and the ecosystems they support are being degraded. Overuse of water for agriculture, the expansion of desertification, and climate change are all putting tremendous pressure on these vital resources. The loss of oases would not only mean the disappearance of crucial water sources but also the collapse of the traditional ways of life for many nomadic and sedentary communities that have depended on them for centuries.

The people of the Sahara, particularly nomadic tribes like the Tuareg and Bedouins, are facing numerous challenges as modernity and environmental change impact their traditional ways of life. Nomadic cultures have historically been highly adaptable, moving across the desert to find water and grazing land for their animals. However, as climate change alters the environment and political boundaries harden, their mobility has been increasingly restricted. Modern borders and state policies often limit their access to traditional migratory routes, forcing them to settle in one place or migrate to urban areas in search of work. As a result, many nomads are losing their cultural identity and their ability to sustain themselves through traditional means, creating a growing social and economic crisis.

In addition to the environmental challenges, the Sahara region faces a complex web of geopolitical issues, many of which are tied to the desert's vast natural resources. The Sahara is rich in minerals, oil, and gas, and these resources have attracted significant international attention and investment. Countries such as Algeria, Libya, and Niger have large reserves of oil and natural gas, while other areas of the Sahara are rich in minerals like uranium, phosphate, and gold. However, the extraction of these resources has often led to environmental degradation and social conflict. Mining and oil extraction in the Sahara can pollute water sources, degrade land, and disrupt local ecosystems. Additionally, the wealth generated by these industries has often not benefited local communities, leading to tensions between indigenous populations and national governments or multinational corporations.

The Sahara region has also been plagued by political instability, which has exacerbated the challenges facing the desert and its people. Many of the countries that encompass the Sahara have experienced conflict, civil war, and terrorism, which has made it difficult to address environmental issues and promote sustainable development. Groups like al-Qaeda in the Islamic Maghreb (AQIM) and the Islamic State (ISIS) have exploited the vast, remote areas of the Sahara to establish bases and launch attacks, further destabilizing the region. The presence of these extremist groups has made it dangerous for local populations and international organizations to operate in the area, hampering efforts to improve infrastructure, healthcare, education, and environmental conservation.

The growth of human populations in and around the Sahara is another significant challenge. As populations increase, so does the demand for food, water, and other resources, placing additional strain on the already fragile environment. Urbanization is on the rise, with cities like Nouakchott in Mauritania, Agadez in Niger, and Timbuktu in Mali experiencing rapid growth. While cities can provide economic opportunities and services, they also create new environmental problems, such as increased demand for water, waste management issues, and air pollution. Furthermore, the expansion of urban areas often leads to the encroachment of human activities into previously untouched desert ecosystems, threatening wildlife and increasing the risk of desertification.

In the agricultural sectors of the Sahara and its surrounding areas, the challenges are particularly acute. Traditional farming practices are becoming increasingly unsustainable due to water shortages, soil degradation, and climate variability. Many farmers rely on irrigation from underground aquifers, but as these water sources dry up, they are forced to abandon their fields or switch to less water-intensive crops. Some regions have experimented with modern agricultural technologies, such as drip irrigation and drought-resistant crops, but these solutions are often expensive and inaccessible to small-scale farmers. The result is that many farmers are left struggling to make a living, and food security in the region is becoming a growing concern.

Biodiversity in the Sahara is also under threat due to the challenges of habitat loss, overgrazing, and climate change. While the desert may appear barren to the untrained eye, it is home to a surprising array of plant and animal species that have adapted to survive in one of the harshest environments on Earth. From the Saharan silver ant, the fastest ant in the world, to the critically endangered addax, a type of desert antelope, the Sahara hosts unique wildlife. However, the degradation of habitats due to human activities and environmental changes is putting these species at risk. Overgrazing by livestock, particularly in the fragile Sahel region, is leading to the loss of vegetation, which in turn affects the animals that depend on it for food and shelter. Wildlife conservation efforts in the Sahara are difficult due to the vastness of the desert and the political instability in the region, making it challenging to protect endangered species and their habitats.

Another modern challenge facing the Sahara is the issue of migration. As environmental conditions worsen and economic opportunities in the region dwindle, many people are being forced to leave their homes in search of better livelihoods. Migration within the Sahara and to other parts of Africa or Europe has become increasingly common. The migration routes through the Sahara are perilous, with migrants often facing extreme heat, dehydration, and exploitation by human traffickers. Thousands of people have died attempting to cross the desert, and those who survive often find themselves in precarious situations, both economically and socially, in their destination countries. This mass migration is creating significant humanitarian and political challenges for the region, as countries struggle to manage the flow of people and address the root causes of migration.

In response to some of these challenges, various initiatives have been launched to combat desertification, promote sustainable development, and protect the environment in the Sahara. One of the most ambitious of these is the African Union's Great Green Wall initiative, which aims to create a vast belt of trees and vegetation across the Sahel, just south of the Sahara. The goal of the Great Green Wall is to restore degraded land, improve food security, and combat desertification by planting millions of trees and promoting sustainable land use practices. While the project has faced challenges in terms of funding, political coordination, and local implementation, it represents a significant effort to address the environmental challenges facing the region.

In conclusion, the modern challenges facing the Sahara Desert are numerous and complex, encompassing environmental, social, economic, and political dimensions. Climate change, desertification, water scarcity, political instability, and economic pressures are all contributing to the difficulties faced by both the people and the ecosystems of the Sahara. These challenges are not isolated to the desert itself but have far-reaching consequences for the surrounding regions and the global community. While various initiatives and technologies offer hope for addressing some of these issues, the road ahead is fraught with difficulties. Protecting the Sahara and ensuring the survival of its people and wildlife will require coordinated efforts at local, national, and international levels, as well as a commitment to sustainable development and environmental conservation in one of the world's most extreme environments.

Epilogue

You've now journeyed across the vast Sahara Desert and explored its many wonders. From towering sand dunes to hidden oases, from ancient fossils to nomadic tribes, you've discovered that the Sahara is much more than just a dry, empty land. It's a place filled with life, history, and mystery.

As we wrap up our adventure, remember that the Sahara is not just a part of Africa — it's a part of our world's story. It continues to shape the environment, influence the cultures of those who live there, and remind us of the power of nature. The desert may seem like an unforgiving place, but it holds a beauty and resilience that we can all admire.

The Sahara's story doesn't end here, and neither does your adventure. Whether it's learning more about deserts, exploring other wonders of the natural world, or even planning a trip to see the Sahara one day, the world is full of exciting things to discover.

Thank you for joining this incredible desert journey. The Sahara will always be waiting, ready to share its secrets with those curious enough to explore!

The End.

www.ingramcontent.com/pod-product-compliance
Lightning Source LLC
Chambersburg PA
CBHW051850130726
47987CB00002B/758